A BRIEF HISTORY
OF DRUGS

A BRIEF HISTORY
OF DRUGS

From the Stone Age to the Stoned Age

Antonio Escohotado

Translated from the Spanish
by Kenneth A. Symington

Park Street Press
Rochester, Vermont

Park Street Press
One Park Street
Rochester, Vermont 05767
www.InnerTraditions.com

Park Street Press is a division of Inner Traditions International

First U.S. edition published by Inner Traditions 1999

Library of Congress Cataloging-in-Publication Data

Escohotado, Antonio.
    [Historia elemental de las drogas.   English]
    A brief history of drugs : from the Stone Age to the stoned age / Antonio Escohotado ; translated from the Spanish by Kenneth A. Symington.
        p.   cm.
    ISBN 978-089281-826-6 (alk. paper)
    1. Drug abuse—History.   2. Drugs—Social aspects—History.
HV5801.E83213   1999   99-22763
394.1'4—dc21   CIP

Printed and bound in the United States

10

Text design and layout by Kristin Camp
This book was typeset in Minion with
Truesdell as the display typeface

Contents

Preface

Until recently a field reserved for sensational newspaper report-age or for abstruse toxicology manuals, the particular history of drugs shines a special light on the general history of humankind, as when we open a previously closed window to the horizon, which suddenly reveals familiar objects under a new and differ-ent guise.

In 1989 as I was finishing a long investigation on this sub-ject—which in the end filled three volumes in small print with narrow margins—it seemed that the probable future of that book was to rest in the bookcases of different university libraries, a summary of suggestions to students as to how to consider the effect of this or that drug in the evolution of medicine, morals, religion, economics, and the mechanisms of political control. The book was printed as Historia General de las Drogas in Spanish, my native language.

I could not foresee that it would later undergo five printings in four years, or that it would contribute to the start of a public debate on the subject, since I doubt that more than one in a hun-dred buyers took the trouble to read it in its entirety. I suspect the majority of them stored it at home as one would keep an atlas, to consult occasionally as required.

But the dramatic gravity that the subject has reached in our times, in addition to the fact that we are all involved in it—regardless of sex, age, or social position—suggests the need for a shorter summary, adapted to the speed of today, where instead of accumulating analyses and knowledge, I simply put together basic facts.

Whoever wishes to go beyond my schematic narration (or to know the background for my conclusions) may consult the longer Historia General de las Drogas in Spanish, which contains a detailed index and a meticulous bibliography. Those who just want an overall view, with main salient points, will be satisfied with a brief history. In any case, I dedicate this book to the second category of readers.

Introduction

A drug—whether or not psychoactive—is a term that still means what Hippocrates and Galen, fathers of scientific medicine, understood it to mean millennia ago: a substance that instead of being "overcome" by the body (and assimilated in nutrition) is instead capable of "overcoming" it while provoking—in ridiculously small doses compared with those of other foods—large changes: organic, or in mood, or in both.

The first drugs appeared in plants, or in their component parts, as a result of coevolution between the animal and vegetable kingdoms. Certain pastures, for example, began to absorb silicon, forcing the herbivores living in those areas to multiply the ivory in their molars or else lose their teeth in a few years. In a similar way, some plants developed chemical defenses against animal voracity, inventing lethal drugs for species deprived of gustatory glands or a fine sense of smell. It is not improbable that some human beings may have mutated when tasting psychoactives, and it is appropriate to interpret so many legends about the relation between eating a fruit and paradise—common in all continents—as an inbred memory about old encounters with them.

In any case, for millions of years, many vegetables and fruits were poisonous and small, such as the archaic corn (surviving still in Central America) or the wild grape. Only with the agricultural revolution of the Neolithic did a nontoxic, succulent grain appear in the cereals, as well as many edible leguminous plants, and a wide spectrum of fruits with plentiful pulp.

This set off changes with incalculable repercussions, since territories until then inhabited by fifteen individuals could now feed fifteen hundred. In some river basins—thanks to methods of irrigation and drainage—the animal-hordes model evolved toward forms closer to that of the beehive and the termite nest: self-sufficient paradigms, articulated above all upon groups based on sex and age, gave way to interdependent paradigms, based on compartmentalization by class, reflected by hereditary power elites. History in the strict sense was born, with the first written languages and the recording of great and enduring events. Hereditary servitude was also born, as were taxes on labor and production, and imperial wars of expansion.

Hunter-gatherer cultures—without a doubt the oldest ones on the planet—have in common an open or endless plurality of gods. We now know that in a great majority of those societies, subjects learn and reaffirm their cultural identity through experiences with psychoactive drugs. Such traditions constitute, therefore, a very basic chapter, often forgotten until recently, of what would be called *revealed truth* by later religions, more suited to sedentary cultures.

Before the supernatural became concentrated into written dogmas, when priestly classes interpreted the will of a sole and omnipotent god, what was perceived in altered states was the core of innumerable cults, precisely under the heading of *revealed* knowledge. The first hosts or holy sacraments were psychoactive substances, such as peyote, wine, or certain fungi.

On the other hand, only time will separate feast, medicine, magic, and religion. Disease, punishment, and impurity are the same thing at the beginning: a threat to be conjured by means of sacrifices. Some offer victims (animal or human) to obtain the favor of a deity, while others eat together something considered divine.

This second form of sacrifice—the agape, or sacramental banquet—is connected almost infallibly with drugs. Thus it happens today with peyote in Mexico, ayahuasca in the Amazon, iboga in Western Africa, or kava in Oceania; many indications suggest that other plants were used in the past in an analogous way. From remote antiquity, the ingestion of something considered "meat" (or "blood") of a certain god can be considered a trait of primitive or natural religion, also common in initiation ceremonies or other rites of passage.

Even if there is a great difference between cruel and not cruel rites, between the gift of a victim and a sacramental banquet, both can be joined by rites such as a mass, where the memory of the scapegoat Christ ("lamb that washes away the sins of the world") creates a blessed bread and wine, body and blood of the sacrificial victim.

It is curious to note that the Greek word for *drug* is *phármakon* and that *pharmakós*—by changing only the final letter and accent—means "scapegoat." Far from being a mere coincidence, this demonstrates to what degree medicine, religion, and magic are inseparable in their beginnings.

The oldest fusion of these three dimensions is shamanism, an institution originally extended throughout the planet, having the objective of administering techniques of ecstasy, where ecstasy is understood to mean a trance that erases the barriers between sleep and wakefulness, sky and the underground, life and death. Taking some drug, or giving it to another, or to the whole tribe, the shaman builds a bridge between the ordinary and the extraordinary, which serves for magical divination as well as for religious ceremonies and for therapy.

It is interesting that in his *Metaphysics* (A984 b 18), Aristotle attributes to Hermothymus of Clazomene, an individual with an evident shamanic profile, the invention of the word *nous*, which we translate as "intelligence." The traditions about Hermo-thymus tell that he frequently left his body, sometimes to reincarnate in other living beings, sometimes to travel to celestial or subterranean dimensions.

Very significantly, the level of knowledge about psychoactive botany depends on the survival of natural religion in a territory, administered by male or female shamans. This is indicated by a comparison between the American and Eurasian continents: while the mass of the former is by far inferior—as the general botanical variety may be inferior—the New World possesses ten psychoactive plants for every one known in the Old. This fact becomes more important when one considers that some of those in the Americas, or similar ones, are abundant in Europe and Asia. But the Americas, contrary to Africa or Eurasia, have not known the great monotheisms until just a few centuries ago.

Inebriation is an experience sometimes religious in nature, sometimes solely hedonistic, which ancient humans practiced with various psychoactive substances. The Ahura-Mazda, sacred book of Zoroastrianism, says "without trance and without hemp" in its text (XIX, 20), and there are also references to psychoactive mushrooms in other hymns to archaic divinities of Asia and northern Europe. The old Indo-Iranian word for hemp (*bhanga* in Iranian, *bhang* in Sanskrit) is also used to mean the trance induced by other drugs. Bluntly opposed to any alcoholic beverage, the archaic hymns of the *Rig Veda* refer to inebriation as something that "carries you to the chariot of the winds," and much later, in the first century, Phylon of Alexandria continued linking it to acts of sacramental celebration; in his treatise on agriculture he affirms:

> Since after having implored the favor of the Gods . . .
> radiant and happy they gave themselves up to relax-
> ation and enjoyment. . . . It is said that thence came
> the name inebriation, because in prior epochs it was
> already customary to indulge in inebriation after sac-
> rifice. (De plantatione, XXXIX, 162–63)

Nevertheless, within sacramental inebriation, it is useful to distinguish between *possession* and *journey* inebriation. Inebriation of the possession type, resting upon drugs like alcohol, tobacco, daturas, belladonna, and their analogues, induces raptures of bodily frenzy where critical consciousness disappears; accompanied by music and violent dancing, these raptures are all the more healing the less they evoke lucidity and memory. At the opposite pole, the inebriation of the journey type leans on drugs that spectacularly empower the senses without erasing memory; their use may be accompanied by music and dance, but it requires above all a conscious psychic excursion, which is introspective at that time or later.

Journey inebriation, which is by nature shamanic, could have originated in central Asia, whence it extended to America, the Pacific, and Europe.

Possession inebriation reigns in Africa, and from that locus it passed perhaps to the Mediterranean and to the great arch of Indonesian islands, where "running amok" is one of its clearest manifestations; in historical times it invaded America with the slave trade, and under the names voodoo, candomble, or mandinga today enlists many adepts.

CHAPTER ONE

Remote Antiquity

The poppy plantations in the south of Spain and Greece, in the northeast of Africa, in Egypt, and in Mesopotamia are probably the oldest on the planet. This explains why their opium contains two to three times more morphine than that of the Far East.

The first written evidence concerning this plant appears in Sumerian tablets of the third millenium B.C.E., through a word that also means "to enjoy." Poppy heads also appear in the oldest Babylonian cylinders as well as in images of the Cretan-Mycenaean culture. Egyptian hieroglyphs mention the juice extracted from these heads—opium—and recommend it as an analgesic and sedative, in ointments as well as orally and rectally. One of its recognized uses, following the Ebers papyrus, was to "prevent babies from screaming too loudly." Egyptian or "Theban" opium stands for high quality throughout the Mediterranean basin, and was mentioned by Homer, in the *Odyssey,* as something that "makes one forget any pain."

Poppy cultivation appears to have originated in Europe and Asia Minor, and that of hemp relates to China. The first remains of hemp fibers (dated about 4000 B.C.E.) have been found there, and from a century later in Turkestan. A Chinese medical treatise—written in the first century, even though based on material going back to the legendary Shen Nung, composed thirty centuries before—affirms that "hemp taken in excess makes one see monsters, but if used over a long time, it can establish contact with spirits and lighten the body."

The use of hemp in India also goes back to time immemorial. The Atharva Veda considers that the plant grew at the spot where drops of divine ambrosia fell from heaven. The Brahman tradition believes that it makes the mind agile while granting long life and renewed sexual prowess. The principal Buddhist branches celebrated its virtues in helping meditation. In medical uses, the plant was the basis of treatments for ophthalmia, fever, insomnia, dry cough, and dysentery.

Not until the ninth century B.C.E. is there a Mesopotamian reference to hemp, during Assyrian times, and it mentions its use as a ceremonial incense. The open burner was already common among the Scythians, who threw great lumps of hashish on heated stones and closed the room off to prevent escape of the fumes. A similar technique was used by the Egyptians for their *kiphy*, another ceremonial incense loaded with hemp resin.

Hemp cultivation is also very old in western Europe, according to paleobotanical data. By the seventh century, the Celts were exporting hemp ropes and fiber from Massilia (Marseilles) to the rest of the Mediterranean. Many extant pipes (and the very caste of the Druids, experts in philters and medicaments) indicate that their culture knew about its use as a drug.

The use of hallucinogenic solanaceous plants—henbane, nightshade, datura, and mandrake—also goes back to very old testimony in the Middle and Far East, although the diversity and quantity of this type of plant is very high in Europe. The Gallic god Belenus—the Celtic version of Apollo, the most shamanic deity in the Greek pantheon—gives rise to the modern Spanish word *beleño* (henbane). Traditionally linked with the sorcerer and his profession, these plants allegedly have powers of causing levitation, fantastic physical achievements, telepathy, delirium, and even death by acute intoxication. Judging by medieval Sabbats, it was perhaps the ancient Druids who learned to tame these violent drugs, using them in ceremonial as well as therapeutic contexts, and also to create philters.

Henbane, mandrake, and belladona (nightshades) were unknown in America until the arrival of the Europeans, but daturas of the *brugmansia* species are indigenous there, and most of all tobacco, another psychoactive solanaceous plant, which is the queen of the drugs of that continent. Tobacco, of major or minor potencies, is smoked, chewed, and drunk from Canada to Patagonia with recreational, religious, or therapeutic intent as well as in rites of passage.

Evidence of the use of the visionary type of plants in Europe and Asia is much less clear, no doubt because of the dominance of later monotheisms. Although *Amanita muscaria* is indigenous and very abundant in Eurasia, as are also some varieties of psilocybian mushrooms (in places as far away from each other as Bali and Wales), the use of potent visionary drugs, more active than hemp, was either hidden as secret mysteries or else later abolished. Only shamans in Siberia and other northern European zones seem to have continuously used psychoactive mushrooms in rituals.

In America, on the other hand, dozens of highly visionary plants are known. Seeds from this family have been identified in preagricultural sites from the seventh millenium B.C.E. Beginning in the tenth century B.C.E., mushroom-shaped stones appeared in the monuments of the Izapa culture, in present-day Guatemala, and continued to be sculpted for more than a thousand years at different sites throughout Central America. Divinities of the Chavin culture, in present-day Peru, shown holding visionary cacti, also date from the tenth century B.C.E. A ceramic pipe in the shape of a deer, with a peyote button between its teeth, dates back to the fourth century B.C.E.

The American painted and sculpted masterpieces related to this group of drugs have no parallel in antiquity: some of the more astounding ones are the Tepantitla mural, in one of the temples of Tenochtitlán, and the statue of Xochipilli, god of flowers, whose body and pedestal appear covered by psychoactive plants.

In Africa, where field studies are still incomplete, iboga is without any doubt indigenous, and it is venerated by the Fang people in ceremonies similar to those of the Huichols in Mexico. The active principle belongs to the same family as LSD 25.

Pure stimulants, based on drugs such as caffeine and cocaine, also trace their history to primordial times. The coca bush originated in the Andes, and since the third century B.C.E. there have been sculptures of faces with cheeks enlarged from chewing coca leaves. Guaraná and maté, both of which contain caffeine, are also American, as is cacao, which contains theobromine, a similar substance. Equivalent effects are obtained in India and Indonesia thanks to betel, a drug little known in the West, which is chewed by one-tenth of the world's population today. In China, tea, which contains caffeine and tannin, has been used for four or five millennia, as well as ephedra, a much more concentrated stimulant. From Africa come the cola nut, a common caffeine stimulant on the western coast, and khat, a bush consumed in Yemen, Somalia, and Ethiopia. Although coffee originated in Arabia, its discovery as a drug came very late, about the tenth century C.E. Europe and the Middle East were the zones most bereft of vegetal stimulants in antiquity.

The generic effect of these drugs is an injection of energy, enabling us to eat less and work more. They have never served to produce possession or journey trances, and were profane pharmaceuticals from the very beginning, used by the well-to-do for pleasure, and by the poor out of necessity. The nature of the effect also dictates that the user be a regular one, resorting to their use several times a day.

The plants producing alcohol are practically infinite in number. To manufacture a coarse beer, all one has to do is chew some fruit and then spit it into a container; spontaneous fermentation of saliva and the plant will produce a low-grade alcohol.

A cuneiform tablet from 2200 B.C.E. recommends beer as a tonic for lactating women. Somewhat later, about 2000 B.C.E., a certain Egyptian papyrus carried the message: "I, your superior, prohibit you from frequenting taverns. You are degraded, as an animal." In another papyrus, we find the fatherly admonition to a son: "They tell me you abandon your studies, to wander in the streets. Beer is your soul's perdition." But beers and wine are listed in about 15 percent of the healing treatments preserved, a notable thing in such a sophisticated pharmacopoeia as that of ancient Egypt, which describes almost eight hundred different drugs.

A little later, in the eighteenth century B.C.E., the black diorite stela that contains the code of the Babylonian king Hammurabi protects the drinkers of beer and palm wine: the 108th ordinance decrees death (by drowning) to "any tavern owner who degrades the quality of the drinks." Rarely has there ever been such a drastic remedy to prevent drug adulteration.

The Hebrew Bible has many references to wine. After the Great Flood comes the story of Noah, who "went naked and drunk" (Genesis 9:20–21). A few chapters later, the disinhibiting drug reappears in the seduction of Lot by his daughters. Leviticus prohibits the rabbi from being drunk when he holds a service or deals with affairs of justice, but the attitude toward wine—demonstrated in Psalm 104, which celebrates it almost with Bacchic accents—is undoubtedly positive. That is why it becomes impossible for one to live by the letter of the law while abstemious, because in all occasions of social importance (circumcision, feasts, marriages, banquets for the soul of the dead), it is correct to drink at least one glass.

Nevertheless, the Old Testament punctually distinguishes between wine and "strong drink." Isaiah and Amos—the prophets most critical of drunkenness in kings and judges—almost always speak about "strong drink," a fact that by no means refers to preparations of higher alcoholic content (since distilled liquors would not come onto the scene for at least one thousand years) but to wines and beers loaded with extracts from one or more other drugs. Traditions regarding such mixtures are evident in Asia Minor—to begin with, the resinated wine referred to by Democritus and Galen—and this practice explains various enigmas, for example, Homer's mention of wines that could be diluted in twenty parts of water (*Odyssey,* IX, 208–11), Euripides's reference to those which needed an 8:1 dilution to avoid the risk of disease or death (*Cyclops*, 145 ff.), and reports about banquets. Since three cups sufficed to approach the edge of delirium, a master of ceremonies determined, after consulting with the host, the degree of inebriation appropriate for the participants.

This basically favorable attitude toward alcohol has an exact opposite in the religious hymns of India from the very beginning. *Sura*, the term for alcoholic drinks in Sanskrit, symbolizes "falsity, misery, darkness" (*Satapatha Brahmana*, V.1.2.10) and will continue to symbolize that in post-Vedic Brahmanism. For different reasons, alcoholic beverages were not welcomed by Buddhism; the Buddhist saint prefers hemp as the inebriation agent, while the Brahmin guards a rigorously closed society, where disinhibiting substances as powerful as alcoholic beverages threaten the principle of absolutely no communication between castes.

The same cannot be said about China or Japan—areas addicted to rice wine, apparently since the beginning of time.

About Africa we know very little, except for the fact that there is no wine-fermenting tradition, but beers made from a variety of plants are plentiful.

In forms such as pulque, the Americas also have known low-grade alcoholic fermentations from the very beginning. But there were no cultivated grapes there until Columbus's second voyage.

CHAPTER TWO

The Greek World

Up to the time of the *polis*, or Greek city-state, the only human options were the self-sufficient nomad, living in small groups surrounded by great virgin territories, or the ant-man of the great agricultural and urban cultures, subject to the capriciousness of a king-god and a rigid caste system. But the Greeks inaugurated an intermediate type of society, where dense populations were compatible with a scrupulous respect for individual liberty. The result was a dazzling birth of knowledge and artistic expression.

Therapeutically, this attitude was reflected in the Hippocratic school, which presented the disease and its cure as a result of natural processes. In distancing his acts from magic and religion, the Hippocratic adept negated the validity of any cure based on a symbolic transference of the malady from one person to another, thus breaking up with the institution of the scapegoat. Instead of using some *pharmakós* or goat to absorb the alien impurity, the new medicine used the *phármakon*, or a suitable drug. In the case of a cholera epidemic, for example, it was sensible to use an astringent pharmaceutical, such as opium, while it was eminently unsuitable to sacrifice youths—with the litany "become our excrement" or "pay the debt of the people"—because that seemed now such a cruelty, as monstrous as it was useless.

Drugs were no longer supernatural things, but—as stated in the *Corpus hippocraticum*—"substances that act by cooling, drying, wetting, contracting and relaxing, or inducing sleep" (IV, 246). Their nature was to cure by threatening the organism, as fire cures a wound by disinfecting it, or as the surgeon's scalpel solves a pathologic condition. The essential in each one was the proportion between the active dose and the lethal dose, because only the amount distinguished cure from poison.

Theophrastus, a direct disciple of Aristotle and author of the first known treatise on botany, clearly states this point of view in referring to *Datura metel* (one of the most active solanaceous plants) in the following terms:

> One administers one drachma, if the patient must only be animated and made to think well of himself; double that, if he must enter delirium and see hallucinations; triple it, if he must become permanently deranged; give a quadruple dose if he is to die. (*Hist. Plant.*, IX, 11, 6)

Nicandrus of Colophon, a *pharmacopolus*, or expert in drugs, of the second century B.C.E., evaluated the margin of safety for opium in a similar way.

The Greeks also perceived the phenomenon we today call tolerance, even though they saw it not as the tracks of an undesirable habit but as a mechanism of autoimmunization. According to Theophrastus:

> It seems that some drugs are toxic due to the lack of familiarity, and it may be more exact to say that familiarity robs them of their venom, because they cease to intoxicate when our constitution has accepted them and prevails over them. (*Hist. plant.*, IX, 17, 2)

In addition to wines and beers, the Greeks used hemp and other solanaceous plants (henbane, nightshades, and mandrake) with ceremonial and healing purposes, sometimes as incense and in fumigations. They also knew about a hashish extract made with wine and myrrh, used to stimulate private gatherings.

Nevertheless, no drug was more popular than opium. In the time of Hesiod, the city later renamed Sicion was originally called Mekone (that is, poppy), and that plant was always a symbol for Demeter, goddess of fecundity. Childless married women wore brooches and pins with the shape of its fruit, and those in love rubbed dry petals to determine by the sound the future of their relationships.

The medical uses for it perhaps go back to the first temples to Aesculapius, institutions similar to our hospitals, where patients were put through an *incubatio,* or healing dream, as soon as they arrived. The Hippocratic treatise on hysteria—an affliction attributed by the Greeks to "uterine suffocation," anticipating Freud—recommends opium as a treatment. In fact, it is from Hippocrates that the name for the plant originates, as a translation of *opós mekonos:* poppy juice. Heraclides of Tarento, physician to Phillip, father of Alexander the Great, promoted it, advocating it to "calm down any pain."

Poisonings obsessed the people of antiquity, especially the wealthy, and that fear fueled the search for an antidote—the *theriaka*—which taken daily would immunize the user. What's interesting is that together with pure poisons—like hemlock and aconite, in homeopathic doses—and many other substances (vegetable, animal, and mineral), opium is an ingredient in all of these preparations. There are thousands of antidotes, each more expensive and complicated than the last, but none lack it; when Galen prepared his "magnum antidote" in the second century, the proportion of poppy juice had increased to 40 percent of the total.

No one in Greece, however, considered opium as a panacea or as a despicable drug. From the times of Herodotus, when we find the first explicit reference to this drug, to the inventors of antidotes, there is no mention of anyone afflicted by its use.

This peaceful use of diverse drugs does not mean that the Greeks ignored a problem of "toxicomania," or addiction, as we say today. The difference between their view and ours is that the social and individual danger of drugs in their case was concentrated on wine. Symbol of Dionysius, a plant god who suspends the frontiers of personal identity and issues calls to periodic orgies, wine came in to Greece as "a terrible stranger, capable of ruining the house that welcomed him," to use the words of Nietzsche.

These tensions are the theme of Euripides's drama *The Bacchae*. Pentheus, tyrant of Thebes, decides that the cult of a "stranger" like Dionysius-Bacchus deserves death, and after a series of misadventures—disguised as a woman, but then unmasked—he ends up being eaten alive by his own mother and aunts, who had escaped to the forest with other women to celebrate in Bacchanalia the fusion of the visible with the invisible, the virile and the feminine, the delirium of possession and supreme lucidity, but then finally to recover ordinary consciousness after quartering Pentheus. The tragedy closes with a hymn of repentance: the god of the vine is recognized as such, and he is to be appeased with periodic public ceremonies. In fact, that was already being done at the time of the debut of *The Bacchae:* four times each year—in December, January, March, and April—Athens celebrated several days of Dionysiac feasts, which did not impose promiscuity but did prohibit the imposition of chastity on anyone, regardless of sex.

There is no dearth of lighter anecdotes about wine. "Authentic and virile" poets, such as Homer, Archilocus, Altheus, Anacreon, Epicarmus, and Aeschilus—who, according to certain witnesses, lived in a permanent state of inebriation—tempered their inspiration with fermented grape juice, while the "cultured and hardworking" poets, like Calimacchus and Theocritus, wet themselves in the transparency and impartiality of water.

The schools of philosophy essentially debated two questions: in general, whether wine had been granted to the human race to render it insane or for its own good, and particularly, whether—as affirmed by the Stoics—the sages could drink without limit until falling asleep, before being carried away into doing something silly. This resistance was of course amply demonstrated by the Platonic Socrates, although the Peripatetics and Epicureans, more realistic, considered it impossible to retain sanity beyond certain dosages. Regarding the nature of the actual wine, even though it had famous detractors, from Hesiod to Lucretius, the norm was to believe that it constituted a "neutral spirit," capable of generating good or evil depending on the individual and on the occasion. One of its greatest advocates was Plato, who in *The Laws* says:

> Let us not put down the gift received from Dionysius pretending it to be an unwelcome gift not deserving acceptance by a republic! ... All that is needed is a law prohibiting its use by youths before eighteen years old, and assuring that men up to thirty use it with prudence, radically avoiding inebriation by taking it in excess. After forty, our law would allow invocation of all of the gods in banquets, of course with a special invocation addressed to Dionysius, considering that wine, at the same time sacrament and solace for aged men, has been granted by the god as a potion to aid in withstanding the rigors of old age, to regain our youth, forgetting that which afflicts the elder and discharging coarseness from his soul, lending him more joviality. (671 a, 666 a–c)

To complete this perspective of the Greek world, it becomes necessary to allude to the Mysteries of Eleusis, begun at a very early time—before the Homeric poems were composed, without a doubt—and which for more than a millenium became the spiritual symbol of that culture. We know that the initiation took place in autumn, at night, and that the pilgrims—called *epoptés*, or witnesses—received a potion *(kykeón)* composed of "flour and mint"; they also swore upon their lives to keep absolutely secret all details of their experience.

Initiation was prohibited only to murderers. Kings, courtesans, merchants, poets, serfs, and persons of varied professions and origins came to take it. Among them were people of the intellectual capacity of Sophocles, Pindar, Plato, Aristotle, and Marcus Aurelius. We know that by the second century between two and three thousand people came to be initiated each autumn. Cicero, one of the initiates, said:

> The Mysteries gave us life, nourishment; they taught
> societies the custom and the law, they taught humans
> how to live as humans. *(De leg.,* II)

The kykeón at Eleusis could well have contained flour contaminated by a visionary fungus (the ergot of rye and other cereals, wild as well as cultivated), which today still grows in the Rarian plains, very near Athens, where the rites were celebrated. It is a much less toxic ergot than that of other European regions, although quite psychoactive; to obtain its effects, one needs only to pass the cereal sheaves through water and then discard the cereal, because the lysergic acid amides are soluble in water, while the poisonous components are not. Considering that water was the medium utilized by the administrators of the sanctuary, we can therefore explain—without resorting to miracles or to the simple credulity of the devotees—the deep and infallible effect of the initiation.

The Eleusinian religion, based on a single act of great intensity and oriented to produce an ecstatic experience of death and resurrection, was probably an ingenious adaptation of older shamanic rites to the new culture emerging in Greece, as a bridge between the natural cults, proper to villages, and the civil cults, purely formal, that were beginning to consolidate in cities protected by commercial development. This model was to have immense success in all of the Mediterranean basin, and under its shadow would grow many local mysteries, such as the Sabazios and Samothrace, or the itinerant ones, like those devoted to Bacchus, Isis, Mithra, Attis, and other gods, temples being opened wherever there were sufficient followers.

All of them kept secret all details about the initiation, and all of them administered some equivalent of the sacramental kykeón. Some, like the Egyptian Mysteries or those of Isis, were designed by a member of the Eumolpid family, perpetual administrators of the sanctuary at Eleusis.

CHAPTER THREE

The Roman World

Roman standards on the subject of drugs were derived from the Greeks. The *lex Cornelia*, the only general precept in this area existing from Republican times to the fall of the Empire, says:

> Drug is an indifferent word, which includes what is meant to kill as what is meant to cure, as well as love philters, but this law covers only what is used to kill.

We know that in the time of the Caesars it was not uncommon to smoke the female hemp flowers (marijuana) in gatherings to "incite to hilarity and joy"—a custom that could have come from Athenian society or from the Celts. There is also the edict of Emperor Alexander Severus, which as a consequence of intoxications prohibits the use of *Datura stramonium* and cantharides powder, or Spanish fly, in the Neapolitan bordellos. Nevertheless, the fundamental plants of Rome were the poppy and the grape.

It is said that following the recommendations of Galen, his doctor, Marcus Aurelius started the morning with a portion of opium "as large as an Egyptian bean dissolved in warm wine." Practically all of his predecessors on the throne of the Empire used daily balms. Nerva, Trajan, Hadrian, Septimus Severus, and Caracalla used opium to relieve the agony of dying and in euthanasia. The same practice was imitated by countless Roman citizens—patricians and plebeians—since it was considered a proof of moral excellence. As Pliny the Elder comments, "Of all the gifts that nature gave to man, there is none better than that of a timely death, and the best is when each can provide it to himself" (*Nat. hist.*, XVIII, 2, 9).

In his *Materia Medica,* the most influential medical treatise of antiquity, Dioscorides describes opium as something that "completely takes pain away, ameliorates coughing, stops stomach fluxes, and is given to those who cannot sleep." Through him, and through many other Roman authors, we also know that the demand for this drug exceeded the supply, so that adulteration was common.

But it is interesting to know that—as in the case of flour—opium was under price controls during the Empire, beyond any possibility of speculation. In the year 301 C.E., a price edict of Diocletian fixed the price of a military *modius* (a vessel containing 17.5 liters) at 150 denarii, a modest amount considering that the kilogram of hashish (not subject to price controls) then cost 80 denarii. Shortly after, in the year 312 C.E., a census revealed that there were 793 stores that sold that product in the city of Rome, and that their combined revenues yielded 15 percent of all tax collections.

In spite of this, the formidable consumption did not create public or private problems. Amounting to millions, the regular users of opium did not turn into clinical cases or become marginalized from society. The habit of taking this drug was indistinguishable from any other custom, such as rising early or staying up late, doing a lot of exercise or not much, spending time within or outside the house—and this explains why no word exists in Latin for "opium addict," while there are at least half a dozen to designate the dipsomaniac, or alcohol addict.

Wine certainly gave rise to personal and collective problems. Romans liked to drink, even though an ancestral custom excluded women and men younger than thirty. Titus Livy tells the story of a patrician who killed his wife when he discovered her drinking, and also another case of an unhappy single woman condemned by her family to die of hunger, because she was found opening the dresser where the keys to the wine cellar were kept.

As if bringing up to date the theme dramatized by Euripides in *The Bacchae*, Spurius Postumus, the consul, persecuted in the year 186 B.C.E. any person related to the mysteries of Bacchus, a cult that had been celebrated in Rome for several decades. After threatening a witness and setting high monetary rewards for informants, Postumus closed the gates of Rome and had some seven thousand persons knifed or crucified, ignoring any guarantees offered by the Roman judicial process. Postumus's words, accurately transmitted by Livy, were these:

> The delights of wine and feasts were added to the religious elements of the bacchanals. When wine inflamed their minds, and night and promiscuity . . . erased any feelings of modesty, all manner of corruptions began to be practiced. (*Ad Urbe Condita*, VIII, 5–8)

Six years later a magistrate complained that "after another three thousand sentencings, we see no end to this monstrous process." In fact, the so called Dionysiac plague lasted as long as it was persecuted, ending only when Bacchus was officially assimilated into Liber, the old Roman god. Looking back, the historian may ask why the crimes imputed to its followers could not have been dealt with in the same way as other crimes; why specific victims (or their heirs) would not come out and denounce them, instead of well-paid informers; why secrecy and torture were used in the process.

Part of the answer is political: the Roman civil wars were to start shortly thereafter, and hunting the adepts of Bacchus became a way to eliminate one's enemies as well as intimidate the public in general; as always, cures applied by means of a scapegoat require suspension of rights as well as of common sense.

But the great transcendence of the senatorial edict against bac-chanals resides in the fact that it was never rescinded, and cen-turies later—with the same disregard of civil rights toward the accused—it was to be used to persecute the Christians, another mystery cult with an exceptional future, heavily linked with wine.

CHAPTER FOUR

The End of Paganism

In a review of data from so many different cultures, over such an extended period of time, one idea that surfaces under different names is the concept of drugs as neutral or impartial spirits, which upon entering an individual "intensify natural inclinations, good or evil" (Philon, *De plant.*, XLI, 171), and in doing so give rise to self-knowledge. Hence, *sobria ebrietas* as a goal, since he who is brought up in it enjoys relaxation with dignity. Philon of Alexandria adds that "those who do not allow inebriation in themselves, considering themselves sober, are victims of the same emotions as the inebriated" (*De. Ebr.*, XXXVIII, 161) but misuse their sacred enthusiasm.

Following Euripides, the pagan thinks that temperance belongs to individual nature: Bacchus does not force women to be chaste, but she who is so by nature "will participate in orgies without becoming corrupt" (*Bac.*, v. 318). Hippocrates already counseled "yielding to inebriation once or twice, now and then," since he considered relaxation to be healthy, healing in itself.

It is best not to forget, however, that this belief—this trust in "individual nature"—reflected a well-established self-medication. The therapists belonged to hundreds of different schools—they healed with music, numbers, enchantments, fetishes, astrology, massage, plants, simple suggestion, and gymnastics—and if there is a common thread connecting educated men in antiquity, it is that of seeking empirical medical notions on how to treat themselves. The flavor of the Greco-Roman world is expressed by Encolpius, principal character in the *Satyricon*, who runs out of home remedies and appeals to herbalists "because it is safer for health as well as the pocketbook."

It is equally true, with Brahmanic orthodoxy in the lead, that there are always those who see in alcoholic beverages something coarse, which leads to stupid actions and orgies. But the Brahmans themselves celebrated inebriation reached with other drugs, such as hemp, and alcohol was not legally prohibited there but was only looked at askance. Even in Rome, a culture inclined to set up ferocious penalties for any transgression, the taboo separating women from wine was not the function of the law, and the violation could only be punished—if he so wished—by the *pater familias*. This derived from a clear distinction between law and morals: if morals were to rely upon legal sanctions, it would encourage habits of hypocrisy, and if the law were to sanction morals, it would become sectarian, encouraging contempt for its provisions.

These convictions—the neutrality of drugs, sober inebriation, self-medication, boundaries between law and morals—underwent a collapse when the Roman Empire became Christianized. Facing vocational individuals endowed with "power," such as archaic shamans and sorcerers, the later ritual castes (Roman pontiff, Greek basileus, Brahman, Confucian mandarin, Hebrew rabbi) have exhibited the professional style of those who are integrated rather than marginal. The religion they administered was also a "revealed truth," but quite different from that administered by the sorcery of possession and/or ecstasy: some were educated and leaned upon isolated experiences, sometimes unique in a lifetime, while others relied upon the learning of creeds and ceremonials, an essential part being a practice that assured the adept's adhesion to a certain concept of behavior and of the universe.

Ritual priesthood and sorcery coexisted for a long time without open conflict in many different spheres: the basileus of the

Greek civil religion coexisted with the hierophants of Eleusis and other cults, Roman pontiffs with officiants of numerous mysteries, Confucian mandarins with Buddhist and Taoist saints, rabbis with prophets.

War begins when a sect—originally connected with archaic communion trances—demands to administer natural religion as well as the prosaic or civil one. That has already happened in Brahmanism, where the old "soma imbibers" later begin to defend an antiecstatic cult. But this can be observed with greater clarity in Christianity, a mystery cult based on banquets of wine and bread, when the Mediterranean basin had been already celebrating flour as a symbol of Eleusis and wine as symbol of Bacchus for more than a thousand years.

In its more ancient forms, Eucharistic ritual demanded prior fasting—as other pagan mysteries did—and after several days of bread and water, a single glass of wine has the efficiency of several. Such was the Eucharist in the Coptic branch, the most vital Christian sect until it was condemned as a monophysite heresy. Many cups found in Roman catacombs, some inscribed "drink in peace," also suggest that the original rite may have given rise to the "boisterous feasts and drunkenness" condemned by St. Paul (Galatians 5:21), nourishing attitudes oriented—according to the apostle—toward "carnal actions, such as fornication." At the end of the third century Novitian, one of the church fathers, criticized the disorderly love of wine observed among his peers:

> They get drunk upon rising in the morning, as if this was a way to sacrifice to the Maker. And not only do they run to the places of enjoyment, but they carry within themselves a place of permanent enjoyment, since their joy is provided by drinking.

The surcease of rigidity, the "relaxation" introduced by inebriation, had been one of the pagan's gifts from Dionysius, accepted as well by the Old Testament. But now it became necessary—as St. Paul says—to liquidate all stimulus toward a "relaxed behavior." That gave rise to rigorously abstemious sects, such as the Encratics, Tatians, Marcionites, and Aquarians, to whom drinking was a mortal sin; according to their traditions, when Lucifer fell from the heavens, he united with the Earth and produced the grape. Lucifer and Bacchus become the same person, or—in other versions—are father and son.

Formalization of the Eucharistic rite began by reducing fasts to a mere symbol, only later to reserve wine only for the priest. This allowed retention of the nucleus of all natural religions—which is partaking in food and drink of the god—while discarding at the same time the substances that provoked an intense psychic trance. Instead of a trance, what is demanded is the wish to believe—in sum, pure faith. Even though the senses themselves may not have noticed a before-and-after difference upon ingestion of the blessed host, faith will consummate the miracle of having the god inside, in physical form.

This turn of events required erasing any point of comparison, any communion not based on autosuggestion. All other mystery rites in the Mediterranean swiftly became "dealings with Satan." God was no longer to have any vegetable mystery or multiplicity; it was to be one, and transcendent, in the same manner as the authority of the faith itself.

Not only were the magical and religious uses stigmatized; all inebriation implied guilty weaknesses. Euphoria, whether positive (by providing contentment) or negative (by relieving pain) constituted an end in itself for the pagan. Euphoria is simply therapeutic, healthy. The Christian faith, however, desired a considerable measure of affliction, since pain was welcome to God as long as it "mortified the flesh": that which didn't relieve momentary pathologic states was seen as unworthy flight from the misfortunes affecting human beings.

Condemnation of euthanasia was added. Each person's life was now not his but God's, and he who shortened his life for whatever reason committed a mortal sin. The goal of a timely death, the *mors tempestiva,* was as censurable as its less harsh agents, called by the old pharmacists liquidators, or *thanatofores.*

In summary, nothing could hurt the pharmacologic tradition more. A few innocent applications, for temporary and localized illnesses, were nothing compared with the temptation of euphoria as an end in itself, added to the threat of orgiastic cults, hedonism, and euthanasia.

These principles were soon to obtain legal force. An edict of Emperor Valentinian decreed the death penalty for celebration of "nocturnal ceremonies" or mere participation in them, a measure that implies declaring illegal any mystery rite of the ecstatic type. In the year 391, Bishop Theophilus incited the burning of the library at Alexandria, causing the disappearance of 120,000 volumes, and after that, the number of archives and texts destroyed is incalculable. Pagan knowledge—especially that related to drugs—was considered contaminated by witchcraft, while St. Augustine declared that scientific inquiry itself constituted an "unhealthy curiosity." Successive councils decreed that drug sellers be exterminated or else sold as slaves. The Frankish king Childeric declared in an edict that the use of "diabolic plants" was treason to the Christian faith, and Charlemagne defined opium as "the work of Satan." By the tenth century—when the church and the state formed a unity without fissures—the use of drugs for therapeutic purposes could be a synonym for heresy. The best-prescribed pharmaceuticals at the time were Egyptian pulverized mummy and ground horn of unicorn, although the indulgences sold by the clergy were considered much more efficacious, followed closely by holy oils, and holy water and candles. The pharmacist was a magician, and magic was forbidden.

Meanwhile, Europe had gone back a millennium. Plagues in the homes and fields, natural catastrophes, privileges, barbarism, and continuous confiscations were added to invasions by Vikings, Magyars, and Saracens to produce a rapid feudalization. Many villages were abandoned; others became isolated; forests took over large extensions of land; agriculture and cattle husbandry did not produce a surplus capable of sustaining true commerce; the mining, metallurgical, and food industries collapsed; communication became impossible or too dangerous.

The prolongation of this state of affairs suggested that so many disasters must have a cause, which was then found in witches, who provoked hailstorms, droughts, and plagues. By that time, shamanic traditions had been revived in isolated enclaves and in the poorest neighborhoods, less frequented by nobles and clerics. The bases for a war against witchcraft were in place, and it would last for centuries. Its connection with drugs is very instructive, but before discussing it we need to refer to Islam.

CHAPTER FIVE

Islam and Inebriation

In the same way as other monotheistic religions, and contrary to pagan religions, Islam invades subjective intimacy, dictating precepts about food, time schedules, and drugs. It does not, however, have a sacred drug—like wine in the Mass—or a sacrilegious one. Since there are no institutions preaching natural communion (drinking and eating of the godhead), there is no hunt for competitors, either.

It is generally believed that Mohammed severely prohibited wine. In fact, there is only evidence that he had a drunkard whipped because he did not perform his duties. Since Mohammed died without further clarifications, his brother-in-law Ali coined a famous phrase:

> He who drinks gets drunk, he who is drunk, does nonsensical things, he who acts nonsensically says lies, and he who lies must be punished.

But Ali was not the Prophet, and for several centuries, Arab judges seldom resorted to the penalty of three or five lashes on the feet. Drunkenness is deplored because it puts a person in a ridiculous light and leads to lying; whoever is drunk without being ridiculous or lying takes on aspects of sanctity and, like the dancing dervish or the immobile mystic, shows an admirable equanimity.

That is why not even the Greeks possessed a collection of Bacchic songs such as those found in Arabic. Hafez, the great lyric poet, says: " I fear that at dawn, on the day of resurrection, your crime may be abstinence, instead of my Bacchic pleasure." In the *Rubaiyat* quartets, the astronomer Omar Khayyám declares that he prefers "the fire of truth in the tavern to the friendly fog in the temple." Among his hymns to wine, we find the following:

> *The grape, which with absolute logic*
> *invalidates two and seventy sects,*
> *sovereign alchemist who transmutes*
> *into gold the poor metal of life.*

Ibn Sinna, or Avicena—the father of Arab medicine—used opium as an agent in euthanasia, and his great disciple Al-Razi, or Rhazes, granted this substance a dominant place in the pharmacopoeia.

In the Córdoba Caliphate, the most educated and liberal place in Europe during the tenth century, the Galenic *magna triaca* was again prepared for the court of Adberramán III: books also appeared there on botanical medicine and pharmacy, inconceivable in any contemporary Christian kingdom. In fact, it was the translators of Arabic texts, in the Toledo and Sicily schools, who returned to the West that part of pagan knowledge that escaped the incendiary fervors of the early Christians.

Taking as a productive nucleus the Turkish and Iranian plantations, the rapid expansion of Islam disseminated opium from Gibraltar to Malaysia, as pills sometimes bearing the imprint *mash Allah* ("gift of God"). About the ninth century, consumers usually ate it, although Persians were already smoking it; it was also frequently consumed in grape syrups mixed with hashish.

In contrast to Greco-Roman culture, which used wine for these purposes, the Arabs used opium as a general tonic, recommended for the transit between middle and old age, to endure the disappointments of the latter, in private as well as in the public *divans*—the equivalent of our casinos. Even if admittedly both drugs become addictive if consumed in large doses over long periods of time, the alcoholic addict has a much shorter life span and greater conflicts with familial, social, or work-related duties; furthermore, he becomes noticed because of lack of coordination, aggressiveness, slurred speech, and the smell of alcohol on his breath, while the opium addict can carry out his duties with precision, maintaining an outward composure without difficulty. These considerations made the leaders of Islam, as well as the people, prefer the inebriation of one substance to the other.

In the eleventh century a friend of Omar Khayyám, the so-called "old man of the mountain" Hassan Ibn Al-Sabbah, founded the order of the *haschischins* with a Ismailian lineage and strong Sufi influence, which lasted until it was exterminated by Tamerlaine. It was a model for the later European orders of chivalry, such as the Templars and the Teutonic Knights, and its members received large amounts of this drug before departing for battle; hence the word *assassin*. Naturally, the haschischins were not assassins but warriors, less cruel and arbitrary than their enemies, the European crusaders, but the French and English chroniclers of those wars saw things only from their own side.

There is no mention of hemp in the Koran or in the Suna. In the Arabic of the tenth century, the plant was called *bangah* —a name almost identical to the Sanskrit *bhang*—and was recommended in the pharmacopoeia for diverse specific uses and also as a recreational drug. Associated with opium and sometimes with alcoholic beverages, it existed in liquid form (as "the special wine" of the *Thousand and One Nights*) and not only as marijuana or hashish consumed by ingestion or inhalation.

The Arabic physician Rhazes attributed to it the capacity to deal with grave cases of melancholy or depression. In extratherapeutic uses, during the classic era of Islam, it was the drug of choice in groups joined by religious faith or social condition: farmers, workers, and urban serfs preferred it, which was why it was *haschisch al-harafish,* "the herb of thugs"; but it is also *haschisch al-fokora,* "the herb of fakirs," used in ecstatic dance and Sufi meditation.

The prevailing opinion, at least until the middle of the thirteenth century, was voiced by Al-Ukbari, a man learned in law and poetry, in a short treatise on the drug:

> Know that Islamic law does not prescribe the use of cordial pharmaceuticals, with effects similar to that of hashish. And since there is no information about its illegality, the people believe it is permissible to use it, and indeed they do.

Coffee was discovered in Arabia sometime after the tenth century. Even though the plant was millions of years old, only then did someone think of toasting the berries and liberating the caffeine by percolating water through them. The legend of Mullah Schadelich tells of a believer overcome by sleep at night while reading the Koran, who used coffee to combat drowsiness.

Five centuries later a tradition describes coffee as being consumed without limit by dancing dervishes in Mecca, who were incarcerated by the Sultan while a council of theologians, lawyers, and notables deliberated on their goodness or evil. The council decided that the drinkers must be punished by placing them on the dock for public exhibition, whereupon the Sultan himself, a great coffee addict, learned of the decision and promptly revoked it. The Sultan then hand-picked a new council of notables, which authorized the use of the substance so that one might read sacred scriptures without getting tired.

Not until 1551, in the time of Suleiman the Magnificent, were legal permits formally granted to coffee houses, and Europeans traveling through Syria and Persia found everyone, without class distinctions, drinking the black liquor as if it were a habit from time immemorial, not causing theological or social anxieties. It was rather a matter of Arabic pride, and combined well with liquid opium, it relegated wine to a definite second place. The poet

Belighi, a contemporary of Suleiman, attested to it:

> It entered the air of the Bosphorus, seducing doctors, dragging them to martyrdom and disorder, audaciously triumphing, from that blessed time displacing wine, which was until that time drunk in the empire of Mohammed.

In speaking of Islam, however, it is necessary to address a period of creative impulse that extended barely to the fourteenth century, and another time of consolidation and decadence. Their great mystics, poets, doctors, mathematicians, and philosophers belonged to the first era, and during that time all drugs were neutral spirits, considered in a manner equivalent to what the Greco-Roman culture thought of them. What eventually took over classic Islam was a succession of fundamentalist revivals, which considered the matter in quite a different way.

Toward the end of the thirteenth century, when the Arabic language had over one hundred different nouns to describe hashish, the judge Ibn Ganim said, "Whoever drinks wine is a sinner, and whoever eats hashish is an infidel." He wanted expressly to condemn several branches of Sufism, which were convinced that it helped one "approach the divine presence." Somewhat later, the judge Al-Zarkasi attributed 120 faults to the substance, including "complacency with marital infidelity, sudden death, leprosy, and passive sodomy." Another colleague, Al-Yawbari, said that addicts to it will "perforate their penises with iron rings, to freely practice pederasty."

It seems that the advice of these magistrates did not become accepted law, although a number of scattered regents paid attention to them. By then, the burning of books and the persecution of dissidents was common. Islam had a censorship in the matter of drugs comparable to that which was to be established by a growing Christianity upon Greco-Roman pharmacology.

These data have historical value in pointing out a change. In the beginning, what was objectionable is alcoholic drunkenness, which led to lying through provocation of senselessness; that did not imply renouncing the gifts of inebriation in general, since—as declared by the poet Ibn Jafaya among many others—to be sober is an attribute of beasts. But on the second instance, any form of inebriation became guilty, because the induced relaxation became not a sign of culture but a forbidden pleasure.

Excluding alcoholic beverages, this was the criterion adopted by the European inquisitors for all other drugs, with the consequences we will now look at.

CHAPTER SIX

Drugs, Lust, and Satan

Some consider that the medieval witch—cooking children to obtain their fat, desiring only infamy—was an invention of the inquisitors that ended up being generally believed. Others feel that they were in fact unusual beings, tending to look for artificial paradises in plants. There are also those who consider them to be representatives of the old, basically Celtic religion of western Europe.

In any case, they were accused of organizing demonic rites—the so-called Sabbats—using ointments and potions. Very few people confessed to being witches until Gregory IX issued the first papal bull against them, granting the inquisitors the right to confiscate their property and belongings. Some time later, the number of sorcerers and witches had grown to grandiose proportions, and the *Roman de la Rose*, for example, declared that "one third of all French women" were witches.

The relationship between drugs, lust, and witchcraft is exact. In 1692 the inquisitor Johannes Nider described an old woman who rubbed a certain ointment in her armpits and groin: "After disrobing and applying this ointment she fell asleep, and with the aid of the Devil, she dreamt of the lustful Venus." Centuries before, in the trials of Carcasonne, the confession of an old herbalist woman read: "In the Sabbat I found a gigantic male goat, I surrendered to him, and in return he taught me the poisonous plants."

In 1324 a document of the Inquisition explained the belief in flying brooms: "While searching the attic of the lady, an ointment was found that she used to anoint a walking stick, mounted upon which she could wander and gallop through any obstacle." In 1470 another inquisitorial document declared that "the witches confess that on some nights they anoint a stick in order to reach a certain location, or else they rub themselves with an ointment in their armpits or in other places on the body where hair grows."

In a woman, the other place where hair grows is that which is in contact with a broom when she rides it. The stick was used to rub or insert the ointment in areas that the modesty of the inquisitor prevented him from describing, the stick serving as a sort of chemically reinforced dildo. The same thing is suggested by a confession extracted from two women in 1540, since they "many times, in solitude, carnally knew the Devil; and when questioned whether they had known some special delight in doing so, they repeatedly denied it, and that because of the incomparable coldness they felt in their diabolic parts."

When inquisitors were absent, the women responded in a somewhat different manner, although the erotic might still remain. Using a certain sorcerer's ointment provided by a constable, Andres de Laguna, doctor of Charles V and Julius III, put a hysterical patient in a deep stupor. Upon her return to a normal, she addressed the doctor and her own husband, saying, "Why did you wake me up at this time, when I was surrounded by all of the pleasures of the world?" And looking at her husband, smiling, she told him: "Stingy, I have been unfaithful to you, and with a younger and better looking lover than you."

Singly or collectively, the connection between eroticism and drugs detected by the inquisitorial mind always came wrapped in stereotypes. From the first third of the fourteenth century, when the Sabbat was first mentioned, its objective was described as "the most abominable lust, without regard to kinship; if there are more men than women, the males satisfy their depraved appetites among themselves, and the women do the same thing." Fifteen hundred years before, an identical accusation—with almost identical wording—was used by the Roman consul Postumus to persecute the rites of Bacchus.

Nevertheless, the Sabbat was more than just pure sex; in one way it embodied ancient customs, aiming to promote the fertility of plants and animals, and in another it was a parody of the Mass, where everything appeared to be dramatically misplaced. Instead of celebrating mortification of the flesh, the faithful glorified it; therefore, the officiant—with a horned phallus, disguised as a male goat—would simulate copulation, giving way to a more or less ritual orgy.

These rural cults contrasted with the use of drugs in cities and towns, which had a private as well as a lay character. Women—especially servants—were caught naked, in a trance state, and upon awakening confessed that they had applied an ointment "to travel." A less frequent case—since it affects a lady of the middle class, wife to the notary of Lugano—was recounted in the Renaissance by Bartolommeo Spina: "The husband found her naked in a corner, with her genitals exposed, completely unconscious. After she came to, shortly thereafter, she confessed that she had gone traveling that night. The husband immediately accused her in front of the inquisitors, and she was burned at the stake."

The painting titled *The Witches' Kitchen*, by the Renaissance painter Franz Francken, suggests how far the women of the bourgeoisie might allow themselves to be tempted by this type of experience. In it we see a naked young woman, and two others in the act of disrobing to rub themselves with ointments; the ladies are well dressed, by no means equal to the old and shabbily dressed witches who are preparing the ointments in another part of the room.

Drugs and the erotic were also promoted by Hans Sachs, a famous designer of calendars in the middle of the sixteenth century:

While traversing the battlefield, they noticed with surprise that the dead Saracens still had their sexual

organs hard and erect. The field doctor—without any
qualms—told them there was nothing extraordinary in
that, since everyone knew that Turks were accustomed
to taking opium, and that opium promotes sexual
stimulation even after death.

In view of such evidence, the use of drugs other than alcohol
was punished with torture and death, regardless of whether it
was religious or for enjoyment. Simultaneously, drugs were
looked upon not as precise substances but rather as something
riding on horseback between an infamous aspiration and a
certain ointment. "If the accused is found with ointments on
his body, subject him to torture," says Jean Bodin in his *Instructions for Judges in the Matter of Sorcery.* This gave permission to
burn people found owning an ointment for relieving pain, as
long as the person appeared to be suspicious or had enemies; it
was also possible that in another dwelling, the presence of very
psychoactive pomades would be considered innocuous. But
dealing with plants and potions seemed to authorities to be too
close to abomination, and put in question the official explanation of things: namely, that the world—punished by God—was
full of witches with supernatural powers, thanks to their alliance
with Satan.

The drugs of the witches betrayed what was eminently forbidden, which is the desire to embrace what is *here,* opposed to
the fervor for the *beyond.* Nevertheless, the desire to again feel
at home on Earth, instead of exiled in it, was what the Renaissance—the animating spirit of the modern era—was all about.
Best illustrated by Faust, the new man preferred to sell his soul to
the Devil rather than adore a God who is in conflict with life.

To do so he leaned of course on psychoactive substances.
The formulas for ointments transmitted by Cardano and Porta
contain not only hashish, female hemp flowers, opium, and solanaceous plants but also ingredients of high sophistication, such
as toad skins (which contain dimethyltryptamine, or DMT) or
ergot-infested flour (which contains lysergic acid amide), as well

as fungi and visionary mushrooms. With such a variety of drugs, and the potency derived from their admixture, a competent European sorcerer could induce various trances. He could officiate in rural ceremonies and supply the urban user, oriented toward solitary dreams and ecstasies, inaugurating an underground commerce of ointments and potions, which—under inquisitorial persecution—would become a profitable target for constables and reward hunters.

The Inquisition in the Americas started with identical premises and persecuted large numbers of natives for using their traditional drugs. It was so effective, in fact, that not until the middle of the twentieth century were many rites related to peyote, psilocybin, mushrooms, and other psychoactive plants rediscovered.

The inquisitor, however, did not find in the New World the direct connection between eroticism and drugs that he saw in Europe. There were an enormous number of psychoactive substances and uses there, not to mention multiple cults, but what was missing was the repeated scene of women in trance with things that—rubbed on broomsticks and horns—transported them to orgies demanding the attire of Eve and the ease of Venus.

The vehicles for inebriation were also different in America and in Europe. After the destruction of the ancient pharmacologic knowledge, European sorcery found itself limited to the local psychoactive flora, which are solanaceous hallucinogens such as henbane, daturas, belladonna, and mandrake. American sorcerers were also familiar with some solanaceous plants, but, with few exceptions, their use was and is restricted to the shaman, because they are considered "too powerful" for others; in collective rites, visionary-type plant use based on mescaline, psilocybin, and similar active principles is much more common. One might therefore say that some Europeans may have celebrated feasts with coarse drugs, very toxic and not very useful as instruments of knowledge because of the stupor, credulity, and amnesia they provoke. The distance between the tumultuous medieval Sabbat and the introspective peyote rites is as long as that between a voodoo initiation and the Mysteries of Eleusis.

In spite of that, it is interesting to note that hallucinogenic solanaceous plants are today classified as useful medicinal plants in pharmacopoeias, not as dangerous narcotics. From 1330 to 1700 they were diabolic incarnations, generating a considerable number of users, creating faith in their supernatural powers, and, of course, leading very many Europeans to torture and death at the stake.

The instrument to persecute sorcery was a proof—the "confession process"—that had been absent in previous legal practice. Alleging the "enormity of the crime, and the urgency of stopping it," one of the voluntary sacraments became an obligatory one, sustained by a wide spectrum of methods of torture. No one could say that the judge was severe, since "it is the accused who judge and condemn themselves." On the other hand, the use of punishment to determine whether punishment was due erased the difference between inquiry and conviction, suspicion and guilt. The new legal principle—that no accused could be totally innocent—is explained in *The Witches' Hammer,* a manual for inquisitors published in 1486 by two German friars of the Dominican order:

> Sorcery constitutes the highest treason against the will of God. That is why the accused must be subjected to torture, so that they will confess. And he who is found guilty, even though he confesses his crime, must be put to torture, because he can be punished in proportion to his infraction.

In reality, the more the witch suffered in this world, the less she would suffer in the next. This also explains why a defending attorney could be denied her, and why common excuses would be ignored. Even though the husband would testify that she slept next to him, for example, this was not to be trusted because "the woman could have been in the orgy, and have a transfigured demon with her appearance substitute for her body in bed." Resisting or being unaffected by torture was not proof of innocence either, because these things were usually due to "diabolic spells."

With things organized in this fashion, there was no way of escape except that of becoming a repentant sorcerer willing to name accomplices, and the judges used murderers, children, and lunatics to that effect. Catalina of Guesala, one among many cases, at the age of eight years saved herself from burning at the stake by denouncing family and friends in the Spanish town of Ceberio, in 1555. The girls who testified in the Salem trials in 1688 were of the same age. By that time, a large portion of the inquisitorial courts had ancestors who had been informers. Some were forced by threats; others sought immediate rewards and later prizes, because the inquisitorial profession was very profitable, and those who were not clerics or civil magistrates could enter it only by demonstrating their zeal as informers.

We might know much more exactly what type of "travel" the European sorcery referred to, were it not for the system that was used to find and punish it. But neither the preparer nor the user of drugs necessarily infringed legal boundaries, and when some authority prosecuted victimless crimes—such as the Lugano notary's wife, or simply the act of rubbing the entrance or the interior of the vagina with broomsticks dripping with ointments—it always used procedures of this type.

During the period of the greatest number of executions, the Renaissance, only a few humanists disagreed with the Inquisition: Pomponazzi, Cardano, Porta, Agrippa of Nettesheim, Laguna, and Ponzibinio. Convinced that Sabbats and solitary "travels" could be explained through natural causes—such as the psychoactivity of certain formulas and the pleasure of relaxation—they denied the official hypotheses of a persistent diabolic plague. This opinion was reinforced later by the philosopher and cleric Pierre Gassendi, one of the great contemporaries of Descartes, and somewhat later still by another cleric and a no less distinguished philosopher, Malebranche.

It was finally a German Jesuit, Friedrich von Spee, who launched a direct attack upon the inquisitorial emporium. After receiving confessions from witches for more than a decade, von Spee made a moving declaration in 1631:

> Treat the ecclesiastic superiors, the judges, and myself in the same way as these unhappy creatures are treated, submit us to the same martyrdom, and you will discover that we are all witches.

An early death saved him from undergoing that same treatment, but the Dutch theologian Balthasar Becker completed his ideas with a book on sorcery, which was quickly translated into several other languages. Having denied the *external* influence of Satan upon human life, Becker placed the hunt of witches, sorcerers, and their accomplices as "a ridiculous farce and a horrendous judicial crime." He was persecuted henceforth, but he had given a death blow to the inquisitors' pretenses. His book, published for the first time in 1691, dominated the following century and was the base of one of Voltaire's well-known remarks, a definition of sorcery in his *Philosophical Dictionary:*

> Only action taken by philosophy has cured mankind of that abominable chimera, by teaching judges not to burn imbeciles.

Imbeciles in the eighteenth century, cannibal infanticides in the previous centuries, witches and their world begin to disappear. After 1700 there were few if any trials, and the scattered attempts to start one were discouraged by ecclesiastical authorities as something "counterproductive." In fact, it was not that demonical energies had withered, only that they no longer conspired by producing lustful inebriations among the people; now they tended to germinate political unrest.

The crusades against witches show how persecution can multiply to infinity certain damages, real or imagined. In a Europe populated by about three million souls, Roman Catholic and Protestant inquisitors managed to burn some 200,000 persons from the fifteenth to the seventeenth centuries and to confiscate the properties of several million more.

From an overall viewpoint, that war can be regarded as an attempt to gain control, initiated by rural nobility and the clergy: two structures in decadence confronting the surge of urban bourgeoisie and national monarchies. Such a grandiose collective hysteria cannot be separated from the great change faced by the West: no one can stop the tendency toward social mobility, a crushing blow to a world based on the imposition of fate on individuals depending on their status at birth. What becomes immediately noticeable in this crisis—the tip of the iceberg—is a conflict between an established morality and a new morality, rejected as something alien, which sets off a cure based on the idea of a scapegoat.

But this is nothing new in our history; it was the same objective of the tyrant Pentheus in Euripides's tragedy, and the same solution imposed by the consul Postumus to suppress the Bacchic rites. Pentheus, Postumus, Bodin, and Torquemada had in common their trust in persecutions which increase that which is persecuted, and produce the desired result only when they themselves are abolished; in other words, enterprises that succeed by failing, and vice versa.

CHAPTER SEVEN

The Resurgence of Medicine

The first cracks in the idea of therapy as something to be entrusted to the clergy came during the Crusades to the Holy Land, because many men came back astonished at the efficiency of Arab physicians, generous dispensers of psychoactive drugs. This explains why, starting at the end of the twelfth century, some solanaceous plants such as opium and hemp were used by physicians to kings, nobles, and clergy to treat a variety of afflictions.

The first references to the "soporific sponge," an anesthetic constituted by mixing equal parts of ground opium, henbane, and mandrake, macerated in water, appeared in the twelfth century. Michael Scotus, a representative of the Salerno school, origin of the later schools that would flourish in the universities of Montpellier, Bologna, Padua, and Paris, wrote that "when you need to cut or saw into a man, soak a cloth in it [the anesthetic mixture] and put it over his nose for some time."

Two centuries later—when witch hunting became serious—the use of opium was fairly well established among Hippocratic physicians. Amadeus VII died in 1391, probably from an overdose, and his physician, Antonio de Guainerio, charged his colleagues in Piedmont with using opium suppositories in excessive amounts. A disciple, Giovanni della Croce, added that "narcotics are to be used only when pain becomes unbearable and all other measures have failed." Shortly thereafter, Gianbattista della Porta was brought to trial for promoting the use of opium in surgery and speaking too much about drugs. Nevertheless, use of opium continued to spread in a Europe wracked by continuous wars, and—as a coup de grace—the republics of Genoa and Venice decided to commercialize it on a large scale, again importing it from Alexandria, the original source for imperial Rome.

In this manner opium was reinstated as a therapeutic panacea in the West. But doctors still had to overcome the public's insecurity about the use of psychoactive (or nonpsychoactive) drugs. Any person without high connections could be brought to trial, tortured, and burned alive at the stake simply by suspicions, well beyond the reach of botany or toxicology. Such a situation bothered equally doctors and drug dispensers, and from that a boundary developed between pharmacology and magic. It became necessary to create therapeutic services beyond the popular arena—as existed then—and more in the realm of the university, with the capability of resisting the threats of inquisitors.

Instead of the philosophers' stone, the alchemists discovered alcohol. It appears that the still had been invented already in Egypt, and the Arabs perfected its operation to distill certain substances; but the production of alcohol demanded refrigeration (the coil has to pass through a cooler medium), a process unknown to Egyptians and Arabs. The first mention of this process appeared in a technical treatise in the twelfth century, which names aqua vitae, water of life, the result of a single distillation, and aqua ardens, inflammable water, the 96-degree alcohol obtained by double distillation.

Although pure alcohol may have been very useful in the preparation of perfumes, alcoholic drinks were given a much warmer welcome. More active than wine by a factor of four or five—and equally toxic—they offered a quick and deep inebriation, reached by imbibing a much smaller volume of liquid, which allowed a choice of various aromas. This, added to an incomparably better stability of the product in comparison with wines, led the manufacture and sale of liquors to produce enormous commercial profits. As a result, distillers formed guilds in the fourteenth century, well before doctors. Distilled products soon started selling well in China, where they created a spectacular increase in venereal diseases within and outside the court, leading to harsh—and temporary—restrictions on their use.

To face the flood of alcohol promoted by distilled beverages, various measures were taken. The most ambitious one was the establishment of a foundation with the objective of promoting sobriety, presided over by the principal German nobles and bishops. Conviction of drunks came along with it in China, and we see that Francis I of France ordered a drunk's ears to be cut off, with penalties of exile for life for second offenses. The Arabs, in spite of their infamy, never applied such severe punishments to alcoholics. Great hypocrisy was rampant, however, and in many cases it was the clergy itself, such as Carthusians and Benedictines, who massively produced liquors in great popular demand.

The Middle Ages and the Renaissance generally led to previously unknown levels of consumption of alcoholic beverages. Chants with Dionysiac influence, such as the *Catulli carmina* and the *Carmina burana,* were composed in monasteries in a semi-religious exaltation of wine often described by Boccacio and Rabelais. The antipuritanism that sustained the use of ointments for lustful and sorcerous purposes had a legal parallel in feasts with copious drinking, accompanied by daring songs purported to celebrate the Corpus Christi or Easter Week. The official documents of Strasbourg prove that in the middle of the fifteenth century the government of the city distributed twelve hundred liters of Alsatian wine yearly to people spending the night of St. Adolphus in the cathedral "praying and doing vigils."

Good wine, however, was used by nobles, the clergy, and the bourgeoisie only. In the home of the craftsman, the serf, and the farmer, it was drunk at meals only by the head of the household, and seldom otherwise. Montaigne deplored this fainthearted attitude with his usual irony:

> To drink in the French style, moderately and with
> meals, being afraid for one's health, is to limit too
> much the favors of Bacchus, that God. In any case
> getting drunk is almost the only pleasure revealed to
> us by the passing of the years.

To mention Bacchus was audacious when inquisitors were working overtime to suppress the bacchanals called Sabbats. But Montaigne was a proper Renaissance man, and he was already thinking about drugs in the Greco-Roman manner, seeing both their healing as well as their toxic properties. Depending on the user they may turn out to be divine gift or stupid vice, harmless relaxation or ruin of health, a recourse for honorable, timely death or for unworthy existence. To reconsider euphoria and euthanasia as desirable is an attribute of the modern age: current values rest on the *individual,* not in any *ecclesia* or conclave of devotees, and the individual listens to his inner voices.

To go beyond witch hunts required two elements. First, it was necessary to reduce the allegedly supernatural to something prosaic, such as the properties of certain plants. Then, the prosaic had to be presented as having great general usefulness, as pure and healthy medicine.

The implementation of the second part was in good measure the work of Paracelsus, physician and alchemist of the sixteenth century. Paracelsus inaugurated a pharmacology that assimilated not only the classic operations but also the medieval findings of sorcery. When he taught at Basle, fascinating European doctors, there were already druggists who dispensed witches' remedies with simple changes in packaging: instead of ointments and philters, they distributed them in the form of pills, syrups, and tinctures.

But this was simple practice, and not until Paracelsus did the legitimate marriage between therapeutics and chemistry take place. A major defender of opium—which, it is rumored, he carried always with him in his riding saddle—he invented laudanum, a tincture or solution of the substance, which provided him with great successes. He boasted in public of having saved the lives of many princes and kings with it. His immediate successors—Platter, Gessner, and Hostium—are known in the history of medicine as the "opium triumvirate." They were followed by the Dutchman J. B. van Helmont, founder of iatrochemistry, or scientific pharmacology, known as Doctor Opiatus because of his admiration for that substance, which he considered to be the philosophers' stone of healing.

The same should be said of Thomas Sydenham, considered to be the greatest of English physicians of all time, who invented "Sydenham's Laudanum" by diluting opium in Malaga wine, saffron, cinnamon, and cloves. He said he never would have been a doctor if that drug did not exist, and that its absence would leave medicine "lame and crippled," that he ingested twenty grams of his laudanum daily, and that he had personally prescribed some eight thousand liters of that preparation to Oliver Cromwell and King Charles II, among others. One of his phrases relating to laudanum is often quoted:

> Among the remedies which the Almighty saw fit to reveal to man to lighten his sufferings, none other is as universal and effective.

The clinician H. de Boerhaave, whose disciples then occupied the principal chairs of medicine in Europe, said that "opium is an immense gift from Providence to alleviate the sufferings of the son of man." This drug had completely lost its previous heretic halo and was now a daily prescription for Louis XIV and Richelieu, consolation to Ronsard, and a "scientific" remedy par excellence, separating serious academics from apprentices and healers.

Until its use became popularized in the eighteenth century, what usually accompanied the juice of the poppy were precious substances like saffron, gold and platinum dust, amber, jade, pearls, waters of precious stones, and similar substances. The client noticed improvement in his symptoms thanks to the effect of the opium, and the therapist found in the other ingredients good reasons to charge enormous fees; the literature of the period, from Shakespeare to Cervantes and Molière, sarcastically attacks the vanities of those patients as well as the greed of their healers.

But opium did not only give rise to a radical difference in the treatment given to the rich versus the poor, as happened in Rome. Its effectiveness influenced a new social prestige accorded to physicians, which reinforced their aspirations to form professional guilds. The first European medical association was formed in London and received an exclusive license from the Crown to attend to patients in the city and its surroundings. Somewhat later, the oldest pharmacopoeias were published, in Nurenberg (1546) and Basle (1561), where solanaceous psychoactives were valid agents as long as they were combined with opium. A review of prescriptions shows that there were few substantial differences between the composition of those analgesics and sedatives, and the infernal preparations of some witches. In short, pharmacology had been reborn—until that time something between alchemy and sorcery—and with it a new industry would ceaselessly grow.

CHAPTER EIGHT

The Discovery of America

It was a surprise to the conquistadors that American treasures turned out to be essentially botanical. The Tlaxcaltecans cured Hernán Cortés from a wound with such expertise that he wrote to the king asking that no doctor be allowed to come to the New World. The same thing happened in Peru, where one of the first deans of the University of Lima opposed the endowment of medical teaching positions "because the Indians know many medicinal herbs better than the doctors, and our experience proves that we have no need for the latter."

Instead of going to the New World to substitute for the local shamans, enough Spanish druggists and doctors went there only to learn from the native herbalists and to sell or spread the knowledge of these plants and preparations in other lands. Their admiration and scientific curiosity were crystallized in the seventeen volumes of the *Natural History of the Indies,* a work of Dr. Francisco Hernandez, the value of which may be judged by considering that the *Materia Medica* of Dioscorides mentions about three hundred plants, while Hernandez's work refers to more than three thousand. This *Natural History,* finished in 1580, allowed Europe to know in detail the richness of American flora and to be astonished by it. In any case, there were plenty of reasons for the astonishment. The Aztec culture, so barbarous in other aspects, maintained lavish botanical gardens, which served at the same time as places of recreation for the court, as pharmacologic libraries, and as archives. In public markets, herbalists and drug sellers were always present, but the poor could obtain diagnostics and drug preparations free of charge in these botanical gardens. We also know that there were several great hospitals.

Nevertheless, there was no way to distinguish between the native medical and pharmacologic sages and the infernal sorcerers, since what some called marvelous cures were for others a work of impure magic. The hesitations produced by this conflict were explained by Juan de Cárdenas in a 1591 book, where he asked "If there exist an herb or root that forces the Demon to come, or to foresee the future." Torn between medicine and Christian piety, Cárdenas arrived at a notable conclusion:

> The man who uses herbs to cure a disease—because these herbs are very medicinal—will not see the Demon or foresee the future. The opposite will take place if these herbs are used with bad intent, to see the Demon and find out things he did not know before. To those, God will allow them to see the Demon, who will tell them what it would be better for them not to know.

The specific herbs Cárdenas referred to are peyote, a brugmansia, *ololiuhqui* (lysergic acid amide), and tobacco. His conclusion is curious, since it defends the neutrality of these drugs but without closing the door to the inquirer: the same potion, in the same doses, can be—as he says—"with good or bad purpose."

After a long century of persecutions, in 1629 the inquisitor Ruiz de Alarcón unleashed a crusade against the natives of Morelos and Guerrero, "more concerned about the good will of *ololiuhqui* than by the inconveniences and sufferings of the clergy." What followed were the burning of seeds, the destruction of plants, court cases, and convictions. Well into the seventeenth century—when the European churches preferred to forget witch hunts—there were still inquisitorial convictions in the Americas against herbs and herbalists; furthermore, even in the nineteenth century, more than one historian presented the original Indian concepts as "a secret society opposed to Christianity and to the government." It isn't surprising that the religious, recreational, and therapeutic uses of psychoactive flora were mentioned in full detail by the first chroniclers, later to be totally forgotten until well into the twentieth century.

Concerning visionary drugs, the New World is still a promising source. If we divide them into two large classes, one resembling mescaline (with its benzene ring) and the other one resembling LSD 25 (with its indole ring), we see that both types are generously represented botanically.

In Mesoamerica, the first drug in this family to draw powerful attention was *teonanácatl* (in the Náhuatl language, "magic mushroom")—a name that covers several species of psilocybin mushrooms. Sahagún and Benavente, two of the first chroniclers, associate teonanácatl with Lucifer. No less deserving of attention was *ololiúhqui,* the seeds of two climbing vines, because—in Sahagún's opinion—it "served the natives to commune with the Devil." The same denunciation was addressed to peyote, a cactaceous plant, containing mescaline, the use of which was soon considered to be "pagan ritual and superstition."

In the Caribbean, the Tainos discovered in Santo Domingo by Columbus used cohoba powder (called *yopo* in the territories now occupied by Venezuela and Colombia) a drug extracted from a plant *(Anadenanthera peregrina)* whose active principle is dimethyltriptamine (DMT), an indole alkaloid with brief but spectacular effects.

Farther south, in the Andean civilization, a plant that has been represented in ceramic pieces since the tenth century B.C.E. is the so-called San Pedro, a cactus habitually containing mescaline, although some species contain DMT. San Pedro [St. Peter] is the gatekeeper of the Christian heaven, and the use of that name for a pagan drug, whose purposes were religious and divinatory, shows to what degree the Indian hinted at his belief under the clothing of an alien faith.

The richness of visionary pharmaceuticals on the American continent is not inferior to that of stimulants, which continue to be the most prized in the better part of the globe.

When Pizarro came upon the Inca Empire in 1530, the liberal use of coca was a court privilege, and to use it without authorization constituted a challenge to authority. A considerable part of the tithe, or public works tribute, was the preparation of the so-called coca breads, consumed in large amounts by the nobility, while for other classes a prohibition remained in force, even though it may have been theoretical. This explains why at first the Conquest imposed a democratization of consumption and allowed several Spaniards to make a fortune on it. A period of conflict followed, during which the inquisitor saw an idolatrous practice in the consumption of the plant, while the landlords insisted on its benefits—a dispute that was settled by granting the clergy a royalty on any commerce with the plant. By that time, in the Potosí annual fair alone—the largest in the world in terms of sales revenues—100,000 baskets of coca leaves were imported, equivalent to thirteen hundred tons of leaves. The Inca Garcilaso de la Vega—an interesting personality, son of a niece of the Inca and the Conquistador Lasso de la Vega—allowed himself the following disquisition in his *Royal Commentaries*:

> Many things have been said and written against the little plant, with no reason whatever except for the fact that pagans in antiquity—and some sorcerers and seers in the present—made offers of coca to the idols, for which reason these people say that its use should be completely prohibited. What is said would be a wise counsel if the Indians offered this and only this to the Devil, but since the old idolaters as well as the modern sorcerers also offer corn, vegetables, and fruit, as well as their drinks, cold water, wool, clothing, cattle,

and many other things, and not all of them can be prohibited, neither should one prohibit coca.

Shortly thereafter, the tithe on commerce with that drug became the single largest item on the list of revenues of the Bishops of Cuzco and Lima. In 1613 the convert Guamán Poma de Ayala commented that unless it was used at work, the chewing of coca leaves was "an unauthorized activity." Nevertheless, its stimulant properties appeared to be very useful to several Spanish doctors and pharmacists.

Another American stimulant plant is maté, which contains caffeine in amounts equivalent to that in coffee. Since the conquistadors were used to so much vegetable idolatry in those lands, we soon notice that that drug was considered anathema: sorcerers used it, as some clerics stated, "to listen to false oracles from the father of lies, Satan." The news arriving at Rome, Cardinal Borromeo wrote to the bishop of Paraguay and to the Jesuit superior, demanding an end to the use of something so "damaging to the health of souls and bodies." However, the Society of Jesus had anticipated the profitable exploitation of this drug—now reaching about one half million tons annually—and was considering the prospect of introducing maté to Europe, to compete with the Mexican cacao and with coffee and tea imported from the Orient.

Very different news about maté then began to spread. At the beginning of the seventeenth century, a highly placed functionary of the Royal Audience of Chile said that "Saint Bartholomew journeyed to the Americas to discover this plant for the use of natives." In 1667 a certain Diego de Ceballos wrote a small treatise in which St. Bartholomew was replaced by the apostle Thomas—the one who did not believe in Christ's death until he touched His wounds—and said the following:

> Saint Thomas the Apostle, arriving from Brazil and preaching the gospels in the province of Mbacarayú, found extensive forests of these trees, the leaves of

which were deadly poison; but toasted by the Holy
Apostle, lost in his hands and in the fire, all of their
damaging properties, and were transformed into an
effective antidote.

The diabolic herb was by now the "beneficial Paraguay tea."
But it is worthy of note that while it was prohibited, its consumption reached very high rates. In the words of Father Lozano, when
Cardinal Borromeo's letter ordered the persecution of maté use
in 1620,

the abuse of the herb became so excessive that only
in the city of Asunción, 350 to 375,000 pounds were
consumed annually, even though there were only 500
Spanish residents.

Another stimulant of American origin is cacao, originating
in Mexico, where the Aztec emperors consumed it in ceremonial rites—in a way equivalent to that in which the Incas used
coca—using gold receptacles, spoons, and other gold instruments
to administer it. The first notice of this substance appears in a
letter from Hernán Cortés to the king of Spain, and the great
naturalist Linnaeus named it *theobroma,* "divine nourishment" in
consideration of its properties. The principal alkaloid it contains,
theobromine, belongs to the caffeine family.

The third stimulant of note originating in the Americas is
guaraná *(Paulinia cupana),* which grows in the southern tributar-
ies of the Amazon and has a caffeine concentration much higher
than that of maté, coffee, or the cola nut. The fact that it grows
in the deep forests, where colonizers were few and arrived late,
explains why this drug did not motivate literature or conflict
during the first centuries. Today, however, its consumption has
spectacularly increased worldwide, and it constitutes one of the
top exports from Brazil.

What now needs to be mentioned is the most extended and
venerated drug in the Americas, *herba nicotiana,* or tobacco, a

solanaceous plant. Drunk, eaten, or smoked, this plant intervenes in religious ceremonies, rites of passage, and daily use from the Mississippi basin to Patagonia, and when tobacco is scarce, many indigenous peoples say that "the tribe is poor."

The first natives discovered by Columbus were already smoking, and we know that the first who imitated them were Rodrigo de Jerez and Luis de la Torre, two of the first Spaniards to step on American soil. They were also the first to undergo a process under the Inquisition because of that habit, because—according to the charges—"only Satan can confer upon human beings the power to exhale smoke through the mouth." Nevertheless, the drug immediately captured so many people and spread so quickly through Europe, Africa, and Asia that in 1611 the Spanish Crown decided to tax the export of it from Santo Domingo and Cuba, shortly thereafter placing this commerce under a regimen of state monopoly.

In the following year, the Virginia, Carolina, and Maryland colonists embarked on mass cultivation of the plant, even though it is an arduous endeavor, which rapidly depletes the most fertile soil, requires constant attention, and places cultivators under precarious conditions until sale of the harvest takes place, often depriving them meanwhile of enough resources to feed themselves or their domestic animals. Months later, the English king James I condemned the use of a substance "the smoke from which evokes the horror of an insufferable hell, full of tar," even though he decided to tax its imports. Before long, Virginia was producing 35 million kilos of tobacco for smoking and chewing.

Controlled by England and Spain, this flooding of the world with an unknown drug did not leave other governments far behind. In the middle of the seventeenth century, Tsar Michael Fedorovich decreed that any smoker must be tortured until he revealed who supplied him with tobacco, and then that the noses of both be cut off. In those years, Sultan Murad IV "liked to surprise men smoking, even in the battlefield, and then to punish them with beheading, dismemberment, or mutilation of feet and hands." In 1640 the last Ming emperor decreed the death sentence for traffic or consumption of tobacco. Two years later, in 1642, Pope Urban VIII excommunicated anyone "who allows himself such a repugnant abuse in sites adjoining the dioceses, and their dependencies," no doubt thinking about clerics as well. Eight years later, any use of tobacco was also prohibited in Bavaria, Saxony, and Zurich, and shortly thereafter in Transylvania, St. Gall, and Sweden. The Persian shah decreed death for this "abuse," and in 1691, the German area of Lunenberg sent to the gallows anyone who chewed, nasally ingested, or smoked tobacco. The habit seemed a new "shameful" one, strange and intolerable.

But following England and Spain, the commerce began to also be taxed by Portugal (1644), Austria (1670), and France (1674). The liberal airs of the eighteenth century forced the prohibitions into diminished penalties or outright disuse; Peter the Great in Russia abandoned torture and mutilations, for example, selling the legalization of this drug for £15,000 sterling to the British tobacco trust. The papacy also reconsidered its attitude of excommunication, and Benedict XIII accepted the so-called "dry inebriation" to " avoid having the congregations see the scandalous spectacle of ecclesiastical dignitaries escaping the sanctuary to go smoke in hiding."

In 1626 a little treatise—*Tobacco, Universal Panacea,* written by a certain J. Leander—defended tobacco's capacity to "elevate in ecstasy and create a communication with the gods."

CHAPTER NINE

The End of the Old Regime
and the Opium Wars

The unity of church and state had now disintegrated in several national states, and the traditional concept of authority had been eroded by rationalism and enlightenment. To replace adult judgment in matters of conscience—justifying it to be for his own good—seemed ever less defensible, and although absolute monarchs might dream about eternal reigns, the modern spirit was laying down the foundations of parliamentary democracies, incompatible with the prosecution of religious heterodoxy.

For our particular story, this means that pagan drugs emerged into the light of day, now protected by doctors, pharmacists, and chemists. They had always been an important means of communication between cultures, but now one can note a mobilization of energies and investments in accord with the progressive control of the world by the West.

Knowing—and fearing—the human tendency to erase its own evil by transferring it to an expiatory scapegoat, the American and French Revolutions wished to establish a system that in successive generations would prevent political power from impeding social change, rousing holy wars against "epidemics" not caused by a germ. This assumed the banning from all codes and regulations of any consideration of magic in general, white or black, since a law regulating magic is a law dominated by magic. But this was not the end of it. Thomas Jefferson, founding father of the United States of America, expressed it with extraordinary clarity in 1782:

> The pretense that the workings of the mind, like the actions of the body, are subject to the control of laws, does not seem to be sufficiently demolished. The legitimate powers of government only extend to the actions that damage others. Millions of men, women, and innocent children have been burnt, tortured, fined, and jailed since the advent of Christianity. What has been the result of the violence? To make half of the world stupid and the other half hypocrite, to support idiocy and error throughout the globe.

Naturally this spirit implied a return to euthanasia as a right, and Jefferson himself tackled the subject in another text:

> The most effective poison I know is a preparation based on *Datura stramonium,* invented by the French in the time of Robespierre.... It brings on the dream of death as serenely as tiredness or ordinary sleep, without the least convulsion or movement.... If that preparation could be restricted to self-administration, I believe it should not remain secret. There exist ailments in life which are as desperate as they are intolerable, requiring such a rational surcease.

Some decades before, in the *Persian Letters,* Baron Montesquieu, one of Jefferson's teachers, had suggested that one "console oneself with something better than either liquor or reading Seneca's lectures," mentioning as an alternative "the Oriental potions which bring elation." No one spoke any longer about the plants or potions of Satan, or referred to the duality drugs/lust. We see the legitimacy of their use for amusement as well as ceremonial purposes, and the idea that pain is agreeable to God was no longer evident.

To return specifically to opium, the first successful preparation of this drug was Paracelsus's laudanum, followed by that of Abbot Rousseau, doctor to Louis XIV, the laudanum or *vinum opii* of Sydenham and other similar prescriptions, with very expensive extra additives.

The first inexpensive opium medicament, powerful and famous, was the so-called Dover powder. Dover was a doctor of medicine who became a buccaneer in America, before meeting A. Selkirk—Daniel Defoe's Robinson—and later becoming wealthy and opening a free clinic in London. His powder, which contained about 20 percent opium, double that of Sydenham's preparation, was sold in drugstores as aspirin and sodium bicarbonate are sold today, even though applied to a wider spectrum of symptoms, from pain in general to insomnia, from uterine contractions to stomach distress.

Illustrious personages openly used the drug: the royal houses of Sweden and Denmark, Peter the Great, Catherine of Russia, Frederick II of Prussia, Maria Theresa of Austria, Louis XV and Louis XVI, and William III of England. A long treatise on opium, published in 1700, reads:

> It makes for pleasant dreams, frees you from fear, hunger and pain, and provides the regular consumer with punctuality, tranquillity of spirit, presence of the soul, quickness and success in business affairs, self-assurance, plenitude, control of the spirit, courage, rejection of dangers, cordiality, strength, satisfaction, peace of conscience and impartiality. . . . Millions of persons will agree with my statements.

Almost a century later, Faust, the Goethe personage, sang a praise to the "enchanting narcotic juice." The drugstore bills of Goethe himself—like those of Novalis, Coleridge, Shelley, Byron,

Wordsworth, and Keats, the greatest poets of their time—prove a regular consumption of laudanum. Certain artists and literary figures, such as Goya and Walter Scott, took very high doses without generating any special scandal; by that time, those who attracted attention were the chronic alcoholics, more or less dealt with by public welfare.

In addition to wines and liqueurs, families had elixirs for cough, lozenges for nerves, laudanum for colic, and opiated teas for insomnia. Although these products were markedly psychoactive, they were taken as medicines in the pagan sense—that is, as a way to combat distress and to feel better. Those who used them in a more disorderly way gave signs of needing larger amounts—a strange thing—and tried to prevent this from generating unwelcome attention, just as any other not quite acceptable habit would be concealed from public view. On this basis, the era of laudanum was prolonged in Europe and America for two long centuries, without conflict or opposition. The Old World at the same time was the largest exporter and importer on the globe.

This opium golden age had interesting correspondences in European commerce. Trade between Genoa and Venice and Alexandria was based on the fact that the silk routes had been exposed since the beginning of the seventeenth century to increasing difficulties: the ruin of the Mongol Empire; plagues; banditry and hostility toward Christians; increased dependency on the Southern route, passing through Baghdad and ending in Egypt. The whole picture changed when a group of Italian capitalists and Portuguese navigators reached Calcutta by sea. This eliminated not only Venice's monopoly but also the Muslim control of the traffic in oriental spices, sources of great wealth by then.

This affected the opium trade because European manufactured goods did not have any demand in Asia, and the only method of payment accepted in China was either gold or silver. For this reason, the Portuguese had established posts in Africa, accessible to caravans traveling across the Sahara, which yielded up to one ton of gold per year—as well as thousands of slaves—and with that an effective means of trade. The system was arduous, however, and they foresaw the possibility of one day transporting opium produced in the Iberian Peninsula and in Asia Minor.

Similar to the fascination produced in the Spaniards by the botanical richness of the Americas, the Portuguese were equally impressed by that of India and China. Many expeditions carried doctors and botanists aboard to investigate the flora. Tomas Pivez de Leira, for example, the Portuguese ambassador to the Celestial Empire, arrived in Canton as a simple druggist, expert in the identification of medicinal herbs. Through him we know that in 1516 the Chinese and the Indians consumed opium generously by eating it. Another druggist, Garcia de la Horta, narrated that some consumed up to sixty grams daily—an enormous amount, two hundred times an average dose—to "treat their nerves," and the doctor Cristoval da Costa mentioned that a certain Hindu secretary took twenty grams at a time without showing any symptoms.

But opium from the Mediterranean basin and Asia Minor may reach a morphine content of 16 percent, while that from Bengal rarely reaches 8 percent, and the Chinese is usually below 7 percent. The difficulty faced by caravans traveling along the silk route had for a long time limited the availability of Egyptian, Turkish, and Persian opium in the Far East, so that when the Portuguese arrived with good-quality material, capable of competing well with the local product, many Chinese merchants began to accept that poppy juice as if it were gold or silver: on a gram-to-gram comparison, it was more than twice as active as the local one.

These circumstances, combined with the dethronement of the Ming dynasty in China by the Manchu invaders, started the first conflicts over opium in those latitudes. The last Ming emperor, astonished over the speed with which the consumption of tobacco was spreading in his empire, had already decided to prohibit that drug, and—as happened with the prohibition of European liquor decreed by the preceding Yuan Mongol dynasty—a good part of the populace refused to obey the proscription; another portion decided to substitute opium smoking for tobacco, whereas up to that time opium had been consumed orally.

The enthronement of the Manchus provoked generalized public discontent, which manifested as piracy, the strengthening of secret societies, and rural rebellions, followed by terrible civil wars in both the South and the North, still considered the bloodiest in history, leading to the deaths of at least fifty million persons. Jesuit and Protestant missionaries contributed to the beginnings of these rebellions, but the ultimate cause lay with the greed and cruelty of the new government.

In 1729 the Manchu emperor Yun-cheng prohibited for the first time opium commerce with Europeans, which did not affect cultivation of the poppy in China. The prohibition was intended to stop the exchange of tea, spices, and silk for opium, in the belief that such trade depleted imperial reserves of precious metals. Since the decision gave rise to corruption of the bureaucracy as well as firm passive resistance by the populace, in 1793, Emperor Chia-ching in a fit of arrogance prohibited not only the importation of opium but also its cultivation in China itself, granting smuggling a big advantage. The motive given for the prohibition was that "whereas it was formerly used by peasants and persons of dubious reputation, it has now extended to members of good families, students, and officials."

This, however, was false. By the beginning of the seventh century, a Byzantine delegation had already brought as gifts several liters of Galen's *theriaka,* or general antidote, and since then that preparation, as well as pure opium, had become part of the official pharmacopoeia. Long before Europeans initiated maritime traffic with the drug, all social classes were familiar with it, even to the point of using it in pastries and baked goods—a practice never seen anywhere else in the world. Perhaps Chia-ching considered his concubines, generals, and courtesans—generous users of opium until the very end of the dynasty, at the beginning of the twentieth century—to be "peasants and persons of dubious reputation," or else we are witnessing a case of double standard, resting on the economic motives described above. But that double standard produced a chain reaction.

In 1729, when the first Manchu emperor ordered the strangling of opium smugglers and owners of smoking dens, clandestine importation—largely carried out by the Portuguese—reached the amount of about one and a half tons. By 1820, when the death penalty was applicable not only to dealers but also to consumers, the level reached 750 tons, and two decades later it surpassed 2,000. After arduous fighting between the Portuguese, British, and Dutch, the emerging winner was the East India Company, which started large plantations in Bengal and counted Palmerston, the British prime minister, as its staunch supporter. In 1838—for the first time in its long history—China's balance of trade became unfavorable, and Emperor Tao-kuang gathered his counselors to take appropriate measures. A certain faction proposed to again legalize its use and to return to cultivation, while another insisted on maintaining a hard line. Before the dispute was settled, the principal leader of the second faction, the mandarin Lin Tse-hsu, threw overboard into the sea 1,400 tons of opium stored in Canton, and although he was immediately dismissed by the emperor, a series of related events led the British to declare war, based on the "intolerable attempt to interfere with free trade." A letter from Matheson, president of the East India Company, to Prime Minister Palmerston is still extant, where he states that "the market was eminently saturated; the stupidity of Lin will increase profits."

The war was to be colorless. The corrupt and demoralized Chinese army was swept away by a small British expeditionary force. Hostilities ceased at the time of the Treaty of Nanking (1843), providing for a high monetary retribution, the ceding of Hong Kong and Amoy to Great Britain, and the opening to commerce of five additional ports. By the express desire of the British, opium remained prohibited, although now distributed with ease. Thirteen years later, smuggled opium amounted to five million kilos, the Viceroy of Canton refused to pay the agreed-upon remuneration, and the second opium war began, ending with a quick surrender and the Treaty of Tientsing (1858). Europeans opened more ports to trade, foreign residents were allowed in, and provision was made for that most hated step among the population: total freedom of movement for Christian missionaries. Although the Empire had surrendered, the importation of opium remained nominally forbidden.

But the defeated Empress Tseu-hi, a known addict, administered a hard blow to the East India Company by legalizing importation and consumption (with a 5 percent royalty), and her successor in the throne concluded the calamity for the company when he decided to renew cultivation in the southwest, to begin public education programs, and to open detoxification centers for those wishing to terminate their addiction. In 1895 the country produced 85 percent of its internal demand and threatened to supply all of Asia in a few years. Curiously, only then did the British Parliament conclude that large-scale traffic in opium was "a morally indefensible enterprise." In 1838 that same Parliament had recommended "preservation of such an important source of income."

It is interesting to also note that the change in circumstances did not multiply the number of consumers, and that the new generations had an attitude toward opium with more self-control, not previously apparent. Chinese historians confirmed the official declaration of their government in 1906. Three decades after becoming a commodity freely traded, there were about 2,700,000 "regular users" in the Celestial Empire—about 0.5 percent of the total population, a number almost twenty times smaller, for example, than that of users of Valium and its analogs today. A proportion of users close to that 0.5 percent was also observed in the Chinese communities in Saigon, Singapore, and Manila, where free trade was compatible with the order and work habits traditional in this population.

For all of the nineteenth century, India was a good example of how the legal strictures applied to a certain drug can affect how it is used. The formidable Chinese black market led first the Portuguese and then the British to establish intensive cultivation of the poppy there. Soon these plantations were to produce millions of kilos of opium yearly, which supplied literally a good part of the world demand because of low prices. In addition to the absence of legal controls on consumption, such a large production led the British government to investigate conditions in India in depth, and the results of this long investigation—extending to thousands of cases, by dozens of doctors—were published in thick volumes from 1884 until 1896 and are known as the Report of the Royal Commission on Opium.

The conclusions were clear. To begin with, regular users—"from one to three grams, or slightly more, per day"—amounted to about 5 percent of the population, while the equivalent number was about 0.5 percent in China. Nevertheless, they did not present any sanitary or criminal problem of any kind; according to the Commission, "The use of opium in India resembles that of liquor in the West, rather than that of an undesirable substance." The report concluded that in the majority of cases, what existed was a "habitual and moderate use which causes no health or welfare concerns."

CHAPTER TEN

The Nineteenth Century

Not only did chemists, pharmacists, and doctors influence interest in all kinds of psychoactive drugs, but also literary figures, philosophers, and artists. The needs of some appeared to meet the possibilities opened by others, within generally favorable coordinates. In the long run, the objective was to establish the power of will over states of mind, using perception and emotion as a pianist employs the keys. With varying degrees of timidity, these thoughts guided the work of several literary geniuses, from Coleridge and De Quincey to Baudelaire and Rimbaud, including the creator of pragmatic philosophy, William James, and the vitalist Nietzsche, who defined inebriation as "the play of nature with man."

Chemistry made sensational advances. Its findings combined with commercial convenience to resurrect the idea of the perfect drugs—*panakeiai*, "panaceas"—incarnated in several substances that successively posed as modern and superior versions of the ancient antidotes. In the middle of the nineteenth century, there were some seventy thousand remedies with secret formulas in the drugstores of Europe and the Americas (the "Tonic of Dr. X," the "Miraculous Water of Z," etc.), which almost invariably used psychoactive drugs and were advertised by all kinds of publications, billboards, and posters.

It doesn't seem strange, because the active principles—the pure compounds—of different plants had been discovered successively, beginning with morphine (1806), then codeine (1832), atropine (1833), caffeine (1841), cocaine (1860), heroin (1883), mescaline (1896), barbiturates (1903), and the use of ether, chloroform, and nitrous oxide (the gas used by dentists) as anesthetics, among other psychoactive substances. It was no longer necessary to transport large volumes of plant matter, subject to decay, from one place to another, because a doctor's bag could carry the equivalent of many acres of cultivated vegetation. The uncertainty derived from unequal concentrations in different plants also vanished, because the purity of the materials now allowed for exact dosages, improving the margins of safety for the consumer.

Drugs ceased to be more or less magical plants, connected with sacraments and rites. The active principles—almost always alkaline compounds or alkaloids, formed basically from carbon, hydrogen, and nitrogen—were understood to be nuclear elements of organic matter: no less "marvelous," of course, but freed from a mythical emphasis. The process called intoxication: was it any different from the body's coming in contact externally with internal substances permanent and necessary for its functioning? And if that was the case, would not its study yield a treasure of useful findings? Louis Lewin, eminent psychopharmacologist of that time, says at the beginning of his *Phantastica:*

> There is nothing else on earth, excepting foods, more closely associated to the life of peoples, in all times and places.

This was the thinking at the beginning of the Industrial Revolution, a period of change, tension, and fierce competition in the name of progress, all of which generated insomnia, neuroses, and exhaustion. Inflationary social and economic processes were developing, with the risks of pure speculation, disturbances caused by innovation in commercial technology, the proletarization of the peasant masses, and overcrowding of population in great cities. A crisis of religious faith and of authority within the family was also beginning, which led some to nostalgically desire a return to old tutors and taboos, while others fell into disarray, unable to adapt to either the past or the present. The increasing speed with which things had to be done was evident throughout. Just then—while revolutions and political restorations were taking place amid an unstoppable technological transformation of the world—all eyes turned enthusiastically to drugs that could influence the state of the mind.

The first great pharmaceutical of the nineteenth century was morphine, one of the opium alkaloids, immediately classified as the greatest medicinal discovery made by humans. Used during the American Civil War and in the Franco-Prussian War of 1870, its capacity to calm or even totally suppress pain transformed field hospitals from locations racked by cries and laments to quiet, silent wards. In 1879 a German medical magazine published the first accounts of morphine addiction, although in the subsequent issue that magazine included an article by another doctor, who reached the following conclusion:

> Morphine addiction is an abnormality which, like the vice of alcoholism, signifies weakness of character. These extreme cases cannot be attributed to the effect of a chemical substance.

About 25 percent of the first identified morphine addicts were women. Later data indicated that 65 percent of them were therapists, health personnel, or relatives of the above; the rest were a heterogeneous group, which included clerics, humanists, people in high society, bohemians, and some prostitutes. Almost all belonged to the middle class and maintained a discreet reserve regarding their habit, although in some of the most elegant European salons it became fashionable to inject oneself in public and to give as gifts special vanity cases initialed by famous jewelers, containing gold or platinum syringes.

Many cases in both the Old and the New Worlds proved that morphine, injected daily with care and good hygiene, would not shorten the life span or reduce one's capacity to do work. Some of those included W. S. Halstead, an eminent American physician; Wagner; and Bismarck.

Diacetylmorphine turned out to be five times more active than morphine itself and because of its energetic properties appeared in the market as heroin *(heroisch)*. The small dye factory F. Bayer became a world chemical giant largely because of the sales of heroin and aspirin, sold in a double package. Overlooking its ability to create addiction, Bayer's brochures stated irrefutable truths about the product:

> (1) This substance has the opposite effect to that of morphine in that it increases activity. (2) It calms all fears. (3) Even small doses stop all types of coughs, tuberculosis patients included. (4) Morphine addicts treated with this substance immediately lost all interest in morphine.

Launched with great publicity in 1898, heroin flooded pharmacies in all continents, where it continued to be freely sold after opium and morphine became controlled substances. Doctors preferred it for the same reasons that had led them to prefer morphine over opium a century earlier: it produces the same anesthetic effect at much lower doses, gives rise to a more intense euphoria, and for several hours functions as a gentle but noticeable stimulant.

Morphine and heroin were touted by Western missionaries to rehabilitate opium addicts in the Far East. Even today, morphine is known in China as "Christ's opium." Between 1911 and 1914, for example, England exported forty tons of morphine to those areas, and Germany ten tons of heroin, equivalent to ten thousand tons of Indian opium. The health plan recommended by Westerners to the Emperor was based on the so-called antiopium pill, the principal ingredient of which was heroin. Half a century later, the plan would be to cure heroin addiction with methadone.

Cocaine was first isolated in 1859 and was soon commercialized on a large scale. The publicity was even more intense than that used with morphine and heroin, since it was presented as "nourishment for the nerves" and as a "harmless way to cure sadness." After hundreds of communications in more or less scientific magazines, young Sigmund Freud initiated a global research project with that compound, which included self-testing, a review of all the existing literature, and the generation of proposals for use. Parke-Davis paid him with the substance—perhaps also with cash—to declare that its cocaine was "preferable" to that of Merck, although Freud also appeared in the Merck cocaine brochure endorsing that product. E. Merck went as far as to attribute to him—without any evidence—the statement that cocaine would allow "doing away with all asylums for alcoholics." The inventor of psychoanalysis was originally the world authority on this drug, which some state that he used daily for more than a decade.

Toward 1890 there were already more than one hundred beverages containing very concentrated extracts of coca or of pure cocaine. Together with the famous Mariani wines and liqueurs, the most famous was the French Wine of Coca, Ideal Tonic, a frothy alcoholic drink containing cocaine, registered and commercialized as Coca-Cola by a Georgia druggist in 1885. The following year, in view of the development of "dry" laws, he eliminated alcohol, added cola nuts (which contain caffeine) and citrus essences to develop taste, and introduced Coca-Cola as the "supreme remedy" and "calming drink." The inventor, J. S. Pemberton, sold his share to another druggist, A. Grigs Candler, who continued marketing the product, adding the barrel container and refrigerated spout: the beginning of the American drugstore.

After some disputes, cocaine at the beginning of the twentieth century suggested three basic attitudes. Some believed that "its capacity to engender very gentle states renders it deadly"; others believed that it was a therapeutic panacea, rarely abused; and still others considered it to be useful for specific objectives and persons.

On October 8, 1800, the then General Bonaparte prohibited the use of hashish in all of Egypt to avoid "violent deliriums and any kind of excesses." The main result of that ordinance was to excite the curiosity of some French doctors. Considering that hemp was a means of knowing the mind and could be subjected to scientific investigation, the psychiatrist J. Moreau de Tours surrounded himself with a group of writers and artists—the Club des Haschischiens—which included Gautier, Baudelaire, Delacroix, Nerval, Verlaine, Rimbaud, Hugo, and even Balzac. The lasting result of their sessions turned out to be a series of articles by Baudelaire, published later under the name *The Artificial Paradises.*

Among doctors, the prestige of the compound never reached the degree of popularity attained by other drugs. It seemed to be a coarse substance, without a known active principle, as in most primitive medicines, even though some physicians recommended laudanums made of hashish as analgesics, hypnotics, and antispasmodics. Nietzsche himself sometimes used the substance and became convinced that it allowed one to get close to "the prodigious velocity of mental processes." But no text of the period comes close to the solidity of the seven volumes of the Indian Hemp Drugs Commission, published by the British government in 1894. The report ends by saying:

> Looking at the subject in general terms, it is appropriate to add that moderate use of hashish and marijuana is the rule in India, and that excessive use is the exception. Moderate use does not practically result in any harmful effect, and the disturbance created by excessive use is generally limited to the consumer himself; there is rarely any appreciable effect on society at large.

Halfway through the century, religious peyotism rapidly extended from Central Mexico as far as some Canadian provinces, a phenomenon that—under the name Native American Church

—took root in over fifty tribes. Some writers and researchers became interested in the plant, and in 1888, chemical analysis isolated mescaline as the active principle. L. Lewin, the discoverer, considers that "it transports us to a new world of sensibility and intelligence; we understand how the old Mexican Indian would see in this plant the incarnation of the deity." By that time, it was fashionable in some salons in New York to ingest peyote following Kiowa rituals, and some of the takers were Havelock Ellis, Yeats, and O'Neill.

Chloroform and ether, at first used as analgesics and as solvents in the chemical industry, were also used recreationally. Encouraged by an antialcohol campaign begun by the Irish clergy about 1850, ether was at the origin of medical prescriptions, as something to be dispensed by a druggist, but a decade later it was considered a "plague" in eastern and western Europe. It was being consumed by humble sectors of the population, since it was cheaper than alcoholic spirits when added to beer, as well as by groups from high society addicted to "decadence," where—as in the Brazilian Carnival—it was usually inhaled rather than ingested; Guy de Maupassant became the most creative ether addict.

It is interesting to note that according to the doctors of that time, "these consumers did not give rise to a much greater number of deaths, thanks to morphine and heroin." It is no less curious that today ether can be obtained by the liter in most chemical supply stores, without giving rise to the least social alarm.

Toward the end of the nineteenth century the first hypnotics, or sleeping potions (chloral, paraldehyde) began to appear on the market. Shortly thereafter the barbiturates, all of them highly addictive with withdrawal symptoms harsher than those of morphine or heroin, soon became the favorite mode of suicide for the desperate. Nietzsche perhaps became dependent upon chloral, and Mehring and Fischer—discoverers of Veronal, the first commercialized barbiturate—died of an overdose of their own discovery after a few years of addiction.

CHAPTER ELEVEN

The Antiliberal Reaction

All known drugs were available in drugstores and pharmacies toward 1900, and they could be purchased by mail directly from the manufacturer. This was true worldwide, throughout America, Asia, and Europe. Propaganda accompanying these products flowed freely as well, and was as intense as that supporting other merchandise in commerce, perhaps even more. There were, no doubt, opium, morphine, and heroin addicts, but the whole situation—moderate and excessive users included—hardly drew the attention of newspapers or magazines, and certainly not that of judges or policemen. It was not a subject involving judicial, political, or social ethics.

Nevertheless, there were some voices of protest, convinced that existing freedoms constituted a "problem," which would deteriorate quickly and catastrophically. The use of psychoactive substances was considered a vice even when it was occasional and prudent, because in reality it was not a vice, but a crime and a contagious disease. This change in attitude rested upon two basic factors:

1. A vigorous puritan reaction in the United States, which viewed the mass of new immigrants and the growth of

big cities with distrust. Different drugs became identified with groups defined by social class, religious belief, or race: the first alarms regarding opium coincided with the corruption of children attributed to the Chinese; the anathema of cocaine was related to sexual crimes by blacks; condemnation of marijuana was connected with the immigration of Mexicans, and the objective of abolishing alcohol was related to immoralities of Jews and Irish. All of these groups represented "infidels"—pagans, papists, or killers of Christ—and all were characterized by a moral and economic inferiority. Other psychoactive and supertoxic drugs, such as barbiturates, did not become identified with marginal or immigrant social groups, and as such were ignored by moral reformers.

2. Progressive liquidation of the minimal state and recourse to enlarged bureaucracies as a response to explosive relations between capital and labor, a process during which the therapeutic establishment gradually began to assume the functions formerly held by the ecclesiastical establishment. The last decades of the nineteenth century witnessed a fierce battle between doctors and pharmacists against healers and herbalists, with the objective of establishing a monopoly on drugs by the former groups.

The close correspondence between these two factors had already been detected in the first calls for "dry" laws, published by Benjamin Rush—one of the founding fathers of the American nation—who said:

> From now on it will be the function of the doctor to save humanity from vice, as it formerly has been that of the priest. Let us conceive human beings as patients in a hospital; the more they resist our efforts to serve them, the more they need our services.

Following these directives, the Prohibition Party of the United States was founded in 1869, always to remain as a minority, but having the support of landholders and even controlling several state senates. Its basic allies were several associations—often strictly female—devoted to promoting temperance and Christian mores, the members of which might vote Republican or Democrat, but would, regardless, electorally punish any candidate who ignored their prohibitionist objectives.

Among the moralists of that period—unanimous in the conviction that America must "redeem" the world—was Anthony Comstock, who in 1873 created the Society for the Suppression of Vice, and fathered a federal crusade against obscenity, which by organization and methods became the mold for the later crusade against drugs. Convinced that "neither art nor science can ignore the Gospels," Comstock succeeded in having harsh legislation passed, which involved the famous case of Margaret Sanger, well-known feminist author, accused of writing in 1913 some articles favoring birth control. Fearing a sentence to forty-five years in prison demanded by the prosecution, Sanger fled to England. That same year, as the American Congress debated measures to control the sales of opium, morphine, and cocaine, Comstock prided himself on the number of "libertines" who had committed suicide on his account, adding that in the United States "some five thousand persons" were in prison for having written or drawn obscene material.

Pulling together all of these convictions, in 1895 the Anti-Saloon League was founded: a very active organization with a membership soon to exceed millions. Its stated objective was to have an America "clean of drunkenness, gambling, and fornication." In principle, the League attacked only alcoholic beverages as "traitors to country and to decency," but the American Medical Association and the American Pharmaceutical Association—germinal institutions then—saw the possibility of allying themselves with the wave of puritanism to obtain control of all other drugs. This alliance was consummated in 1903, when plenary sessions of both corporations declared that "who kills the body of a man is an angel, compared to he who destroys the soul of another, by administering a drug without prescription, not sold in a pharmacy"; morphine, for example, had a "diabolic power, transmutable into a blessing if dispensed by therapists with a diploma." Two years later, when opium and morphine were the fourth bestselling pharmaceuticals in the United States, some leaders of those associations began to declare that their free sale converted young people into criminals and prostitutes—a prophecy that would have to await Prohibition before becoming fact.

Few could imagine that two decades later both associations—the medical and the pharmaceutical—were to denounce before Congress "a conspiracy to remove their accustomed rights from the therapeutic professions," since almost thirty thousand doctors and some eight thousand pharmacists were in jail for prescribing or dispensing opium and morphine to undercover policemen disguised as addicts.

But this alliance between therapists and puritans was crystallized in laws because it related to the expansion of American power over the globe, added to the tireless activity of three men. The first was the Reverend W. S. Crafts, a high official in the administration of Theodore Roosevelt, who in the World Missionary Conference (1900) proposed to celebrate the start of the second Christian millennium with an "international civilizing crusade against alcohol and drugs"; its purpose was "a policy of prohibition in all indigenous races, in the interests of commerce as well as conscience."

The second was Charles H. Brent, first bishop of Manila after the annexation of the Philippine archipelago by the Americans, whose main aim in life was to "free Asia from opium." With the assistance of the Methodist bishop H. Stunz of Manila as well, and by pressure applied by Crafts upon Roosevelt, Brent secured a prohibition against "all nonmedical use" of opium in the Philippines, offering free treatment—mainly with the "antiopium pill"—to anyone who wished to abandon the vice.

The third decisive notable was H. Wright, a young man of great energy and political ambition, whose only problem was alcoholism. Even though President Wilson eventually fired him for that reason, no one did more for the prohibition of opium and cocaine in the United States, since he designed the procedure to advance the cause without requiring a constitutional amendment. The strategy was to successively present to Congress projects for international agreements as a base for then requesting the passage of American regulations to conform with such agreements. Even though at first this strategy was not particularly successful—two proposed laws were rejected—Wright saw his efforts crowned with success with the Harrison Act, passed the same year that he was terminated.

The efforts of these reformers coincided with a difficult phase in the relations between the United States and China, to such a degree that Roosevelt wanted to send a detachment of marines to protect American investments in China. A peaceful solution was also possible, and nothing would be better, Brent told him, than to start "by helping China in its battle against opium." Wright wrote to the secretary of state: "This initiative can be used as oil to calm down the turbulent waters there caused by our aggressive commercial policies." Crafts also intensified his support of the initiative; as Bishop Stunz had mentioned, "at least 30 million Americans demand such a gesture." Abandoning the project of requesting funds for an invasion, the President thought that he might, with much less money, call together an international conference on opium, and benefit from that delay by negotiating economic interests.

In that way, a commission formed by Brent, Wright, and C. C. Tenney, a missionary, called together the Shanghai Conference in 1906. Twelve countries attended, and the delegates were reluctant to start a crusade against nonmedical uses of that drug. Instead of "resolutions," the American delegation—Brent, Wright, and Tenney—could only secure vague "recommendations" (such as attempting the gradual suppression of *smoked* opium), which Wright considered "disappointing" in private, and "a great success" when he reported before Congress. But Shanghai was the germ of future meetings, where an ever stronger America insisted on being heard more. Three days before the start of World War I, The Hague Convention was signed (1914), proposing that all nations "control the preparation and distribution of opium, morphine, and cocaine." This agreement, incorporated as a provision of the Treaty of Versailles (1919), set the precedent that it is the right—and the duty—of all states to watch over the "legitimate use" of certain drugs.

The zeal of these reformers was in part a true reflection of the situation in North America. In 1914 it was illegal to smoke tobacco in twelve states, and it would soon be so in twenty-eight. Restrictions on the consumption of alcohol increased daily and became more severe. It was precisely then that the federal Congress approved a strange law, because it was presented as an administrative regulation—it demanded registration in certain offices of every manufacturer, distributor, or possessor of opium, morphine, and cocaine— but was in fact a substantial penal regulation, aiming to eliminate all "nonmedical" uses of such materials, and granted ultimate authority to define what was and was not "medical" to a new entity: the Narcotics Control Department. Just one week after approving that precept, the Harrison Act, Congress received a petition to establish "dry" laws signed by six million people.

Had it not been for this ingenious solution, the crusade against opium, morphine, and cocaine would have had to repeat the intricate steps followed by the antialcohol crusade that led to the eighteenth amendment. To what degree the phrasing of the Harrison Act deceived the American therapeutic establishment is evident by the endorsement given the law by both the American Medical Association and the American Pharmaceutical Association, even though they attempted to clarify, by editorials in their respective journals, that it would be unconstitutional to interpret the law as "ceding police powers" to persons other than doctors or pharmacists. In the final analysis, none of the law's provisions mention changing the pharmacopoeia by eliminating these three drugs from it.

Lurking behind the whitewash of a postal-registration law,

nevertheless, was the aim of wiping out those three agents of euphoria, as well as with any other ones that might "create or excite antinatural appetites," as Wright put it. Forced to deal with the first trials, the Supreme Court deliberated for five years over the constitutionality of the Harrison Act, absolving persons accused of violating it until 1919—the same year when the prohibition laws were approved—when the justices gave way to prohibitionist sentiments with two convictions. One condemned a doctor for prescribing five hundred vials of morphine to his patient, and another declared a course of maintenance therapy to be "a semantic perversion, unworthy of a doctor." Weeks later, the director of the Narcotics Control Department stated his "justification to revoke the authority of doctors and pharmacists." The crusade marched on and affected alcohol as well as derivatives of the poppy and of coca.

In 1905 when the first voices of alarm were heard, Congress created a special committee to evaluate the number of "users" of opiates and cocaine in the United States. Its conclusions were that there might be two hundred thousand persons—about 0.5 percent of the population then—but that the rate of increase in imports implied a rapid enlargement of that number in the future.

Opium and morphine users were largely persons of middle age and older, well integrated socially and in their work, who had started using these drugs under medical recommendation and had been using them for a decade or more. Cocaine lovers were not as old, nor were they prominent in their excesses of use; between 1906 and 1914, Georgia, the state theoretically most afflicted by abuse of the drug by blacks, registered only two cases of persons who had come to a clinic for treatment of their habit.

Of course, in that report not a single instance of death by accidental overdose is mentioned, and neither are crimes committed under the influence of opium or morphine. Some of the documentation reviewed by the special committee included some newspaper articles from the South, with reports about the increase in sexual aggression inflicted upon white women by colored men under the influence of cocaine (basically thanks to

Coca-Cola), but the senators did not consider that this material proved anything.

In 1919 another committee charged by Congress to evaluate the number of users (now classified as "addicts") estimated that number to be 238,000, indicating that the rate of growth had not been foreseen in 1905, and that it was indeed lower than the rate of growth of the total population. In this report as well, no cases of overdose are mentioned, or of crimes committed by addicts. With drugs available in pharmacies and drugstores, there were simply no cases of *accidental* overdose (suicides excluded), nor did there appear to be any encouragement to crime among users. But in 1919 America was inflamed with prohibitionist fervor, and the 238,000 number appeared to be "monstrous."

Armed with repressive legislation, and convinced that the quarter million persons "would wish to stop taking drugs, as long as it is made difficult for them," the crusaders designed a system that basically consisted of disguising policemen as users and infiltrating them into medical offices and drugstores. If opium, morphine, or cocaine was generously prescribed or dispensed in any of those locations, the doctor or pharmacist was brought to trial as "conspiring to violate the Harrison Act," and thus forty thousand professionals went to prison between 1920 and 1930. But before the end of the decade—by which time more than eighty thousand people were serving jail sentences for this reason—certain reactions began to appear. Smuggling increased wildly, some policemen were convicted for blackmail, and the type of user changed: whereas formerly the user was usually from the middle class and forty years or older, without a criminal record, use now became centered in much younger persons, with lower incomes, often with criminal records and therefore having greater access to the black market.

The Volstead Act, generally known in Europe as the "dry law," became effective at the beginning of 1920 with the express purpose of "creating a new nation." Senator Volstead himself at that time broadcast a message through the newspapers and radio, saying among other things:

> The poor sections of cities will soon be a thing of
> the past. Prisons and correctional institutions will be
> empty. All men will walk with their heads high, all
> women will smile, all children will laugh. The doors
> of hell will forever be closed.

This law provided fines and prison sentences for the sale and manufacture of alcoholic beverages—six months for the first offense, and five years for the second—as well as closure for one year of any establishment where consumption took place, "excepting wine for the Holy Mass." Medical use of alcohol was also excepted, provided the doctor was registered on a special list—where, incidentally, over a hundred thousand doctors soon signed up.

By 1932, twelve years after its effective date, the law had created a half million new delinquents and led to corruption at all levels. A good 34 percent of prohibition agents have unfavorable reports in their personnel files; 11 percent are convicted of "extortion, theft, creating fraudulent evidence, robbery, trafficking, and personal damage." Two secretaries—of the Department of Interior and the Department of Justice—had been convicted on account of gang connections and contraband. Almost thirty thousand had died from drinking methyl alcohol and other toxic distillations, and some hundred thousand suffered from permanent damage such as blindness or paralysis. Three great "families"—Jews, Irish, and Italians—between themselves enjoyed the monopoly of violating the Volstead Act, while regular drinkers had the difficult choice of either attending clandestine saloons or going to a doctor to secure a prescription for whisky, cognac, or wine at a considerably higher price.

The "dry" law, or Prohibition, was terminated in 1933, in view of the fact that it had produced "injustice, hypocrisy, criminalization of large segments of society, overwhelming corruption, and creation of organized crime." The three "families," until then separated by fierce rivalries, agreed on a policy of peaceful coexistence: a prudent step in the face of imminent ruin that the end of Prohibition represented for them.

It was then that the leaders of the Jewish and Italian gangs, M. Lansky and S. Luciano, studied the possibility of diverting their interest to morphine and cocaine, benefiting from the proscription in place for those drugs. Cocaine was useless, because in that same year amphetamine, a much more active stimulant, was introduced into commerce and freely sold in drugstores; and morphine, with a limited capacity for euphoria, was still associated with orderly people. But American legislators had seen to it to make illegal the production and sale of heroin—until that time used as a cure for opium and morphine addicts—and it was here that the desolate gangsters found their salvation.

CHAPTER TWELVE

The Beginnings
of the Crusade

E̶ven though the Volstead Act made more than half a million people criminals, it did not result in the conviction of the big producers or traffickers in alcoholic beverages; we must remember that Capone was not convicted as a smuggler or an owner of illegal establishments, but for fiscal fraud. With hired killers and corrupt lawyers in his service, amply supported by some politicians, the heads of these enterprises remained outside the reach of the law. That is why the end of Prohibition produced discomfort among gangsters similar to that afflicting puritan circles, as well great celebration among imbibers. Following the lead of many senators and representatives, Commissioner Elliot Ness—mortal enemy of smugglers and peddlers of alcohol—decided to celebrate by "having a drink," incidentally celebrating the end of the Great Depression as well. That took place during the first term of President Franklin D. Roosevelt, known for a progressive spirit more open to European trends than to American reformist attitudes.

With the abolishment of Prohibition, the future of the

Harrison Act and its practical banning of opium, morphine, and cocaine in the United States had to be determined. Also, the status of international drug legislation had to be addressed. Even though the problem was nonexistent in Europe and the rest of the world, the situation in the United States was not that simple. Criminal associations that had emerged under the Volstead Act remained fully in place, now threatened by imminent ruin; there also existed an institutional mechanism charged with repressing the use of drugs, a medical establishment mired in doubts, a chemical industry based on successive synthetic derivatives of morphine and cocaine, and, finally, a group of dedicated users.

The combined effect of these factors determined the future to come. By 1930 those who used opium and morphine daily continued to belong to an older group, or at least an upper-middle-aged one. Two rigorous surveys—the first made by Lawrence Kolb, who later became surgeon general, and the second sponsored by the American Medical Association—indicated that the habit was compatible even with the correct performance of domestic, social, and work duties, and that it was not the exception, but the rule, that cases of thirty and even sixty years of daily use involved doctors and other professionals whose performances were competent, as well as exemplary mothers.

American clinic directors, internists, and toxicologists soon protested the fact that it was now policemen who were resolving questions about how much and when to prescribe certain drugs. Following the steps taken by Dr. E. Bishop, several colleagues initiated a counterattack, and in 1921 an editorial in the *Medical Record* of New York denounced the increasing "slavery of the medical profession"; in that same year, the *Journal of the American Medical Association* published another virulent article affirming that "the press corrupts public opinion deliberately and systematically, presenting the habit of taking certain drugs as a disease." To attempt to cure a vice by calling it a disease and a criminal act is to certainly assure that it becomes a disease and a crime. Dressed as benevolence and scientific orientation, the practice of fighting pain in some persons by making the best remedies illegal is equivalent to cruelty and superstition, since the really damaging circumstance for someone addicted to opiates is having to undergo periodic withdrawal episodes. Bishop insisted that the narcotics "problem" was an invention of Prohibition, with the aim of creating a "moral stigma" around the user of certain drugs: a practice he considered "barbarous, damaging and useless." The intensity of this polemic is visible in an article published by another doctor, R. A. Schless, published by the *American Mercury* in 1925:

> The largest part of drug addiction today is due to the Harrison Act, which prohibited the sale of narcotics without medical prescription. . . . Ruined addicts act as provocatory agents for distributors, being rewarded with outright gifts of the substances, or with deliveries on credit. The Harrison Act created drug traffickers, and traffickers create addicts.

Shortly thereafter, a high-ranking police official admitted in public "the justified complaint of doctors against our agents, since some have accosted them with blackmail, attempting to improve their service records at the doctors' expense." Bishop himself was brought to trial for prescribing twenty doses of morphine to an undercover policeman. The practice of pretending addiction to obtain a prescription, and later to denounce or blackmail the doctor, became so prevalent that in 1932 Dr. J. Volk, a House representative, denounced before Congress a "conspiracy to deprive the medical profession of its customary rights, by means of an unconstitutional law, interpreted unconstitutionally." The Supreme Court did not ignore it, and two decisions placed the legitimacy of the Harrison Act into question, leading the executive branch to ask Congress for a constitutional amendment confirming its powers.

But the medical establishment did not lend its support to such an initiative in the thirties, as it had two decades before. Lawyers' associations expressly opposed it, and the ensuing deliberations necessary to move a constitutional amendment forward would have required the airing of scarcely encouraging data, especially in a nation that had just abolished the prohibition of alcohol. These data included the increasing corruption prevalent in sellers and enforcement agents, a 400 percent increase in smuggling, and discouraging results from forced rehabilitation efforts: out of some 100,000 people imprisoned until then by virtue of the Harrison Act, fewer than 3 percent remained abstemious five years after being released. To be exact, in 1928 one-third of male and female prison inmates were there because of opiates and cocaine, provoking a saturation that gave rise to the "narcotic farms" of Fort Worth and Lexington—institutions midway between prisons and concentration camps. The picture was rounded out by a recent scandal, since the murder of a mafioso revealed the bribe accepted by the son and the son-in-law of the narcotics chief, R. Levi Nutt.

The timing was wrong for the introduction of a new constitutional amendment but right for the "American heartland" to close ranks, and so it did. General W. B. Wheeler, president of the Anti-Saloon League, declared to Congress that "the need for the Harrison Act has been proven by the very same difficulties of its application," and many other associations, such as the Federation of Women's Clubs, threw in their support. The Supreme Court responded to this pressure and that of the executive branch by a decision passed by simple majority, which accepted the constitutionality of the precept. The previous narcotics chief was replaced by H. J. Anslinger, former secret agent and old antialcohol policeman who remained in his post for three decades. A convinced believer in repressive measures, Anslinger succeeded in declaring marijuana illegal and in gradually adding other natural and synthetic substances to the list of the four originally prohibited.

The Marijuana Tax Act of 1937 had something in common with the Harrison Act: it was not a substantial penal regulation, and as such it did not require a constitutional amendment, even though for practical purposes it was a way of classifying as a crime the production, dispensing, or possession of hemp. Anslinger had put together a dossier with protests by neighborhood associations against Mexican users of marijuana, to support his contention that that substance produced "unstoppable outbreaks of violence and lust." The day before the hearing, Anslinger had declared to the press:

> It is almost impossible to estimate the number of murders, suicides, thefts, muggings, extortion, and misdemeanors of manic insanity provoked by marijuana each year.

Dr. W. I. Treadway, representing the Division of Mental Health, and Dr. W. Woodward, from the American Medical Association, refuted these claims before Congress, referring to ancient traditions of peaceful and moderate use as well as to all of the available scientific literature. Similar defenses were attested by a thick report commissioned by the mayor of New York City, which denied any addictive nature of marijuana and stated that it did not produce tendencies to commit criminal acts (a report that, incidentally, mysteriously disappeared for some thirty years), as well as two studies initiated by the U.S. Army in 1932 and 1933 dealing with army personnel stationed in Panama, which concluded that "it was not desirable to prohibit the use or the sale of marijuana." Anslinger's thesis was contradicted as well by a study completed in 1934 by the district attorney of New Orleans, where 75,000 crimes and 75,000 cases were reviewed and no cause-and-effect relationship could be established between consumption of marijuana and murders, physical aggression, rapes, or dishonest abuses.

Even then, the Marijuana Tax Act was unanimously approved; unanimity, a very infrequent circumstance in American legislative practice, was to characterize all laws about drugs passed by Congress for the next three decades. Dr. Woodward, who had participated in the hearing representing the American Medical Association and was prominently opposed to the concept, soon thereafter fell victim of a police trap and was accused of "illicit practices."

While the medical, judicial, and enforcement establishments were engaged in these complex relationships in the United States, a part of the rest of the world began to welcome the idea that pharmacologic consumption was a matter of concern to the state. The absence of conflict in this field presented the North American initiative as a strictly scientific matter, which in practice translated into limiting the dispensing of opium, morphine, and cocaine to pharmacies and demanding medical prescriptions for any preparations containing high concentrations of such drugs. This had been the spirit evident in The Hague Conventions of 1912, 1913 and 1914, initially endorsed by eight nations and later endorsed by most of them, thanks to its placement as fine print in the Treaty of Versailles in 1919, which put an end to World War I. The United States, the main victorious power, did not support such a lukewarm regulation—which made recommendations rather than adopted resolutions, and which retained the free sale of preparations containing small amounts of the controlled drugs—but the American delegation trusted the future.

With this in mind, a conference was called in 1925 in Geneva, where the American delegation abruptly departed in anger before it was concluded. The American objective was not to stop with the control of manufactured products but also to put limits on the amount of crude opium and coca produced in each area of the globe. The proposal was not accepted by the other delegations gathered in Geneva, who considered the fact that the United States was in the middle of Prohibition required a wait-and-see posture. When the Americans departed from the conference, the rest of the delegations agreed on a position similar to that stated at The Hague, changing the phrase "medical and legitimate uses" to "medical and scientific uses," thus reducing the ambivalence attached to *legitimate*. The first novelty at the convention was the creation of a consultative international body, the Central Permanent Committee, to "keep an eye on the drug market." The second novelty was to extend the mechanisms of control to heroin and hemp, not mentioned at The Hague. The restriction of marijuana and hashish to "medical and scientific uses" was due to pressures applied by the Italian delegation, because even though the British Army had made a monumental study some decades earlier about the use of this drug in India, which concluded that its free sale should be continued, hashish had by then lately become a symbol of anticolonial subversion in Egypt, which had just become a kingdom though continuing de facto to be a British protectorate.

Apart from that, the Geneva Conference did not depart from The Hague agreements. The signatories undertook not to export controlled drugs to countries where they were prohibited (only the United States was in that position at that time) and to study the "possibility" of passing internal regulations to punish illicit traffic. Infractions were to be dealt with by "confiscation" of the shipment. This was not enough punishment and was described as "a joke" by the American delegation, but it did in fact reflect social realities in other countries. In the case of Spain, a signatory of The Hague and Geneva conventions, from 1920 to 1930, during which time pharmacies were dispensing opium, morphine, and cocaine with and without prescriptions, there were only six cases of lethal overdose with these drugs, five of them being suicides and the only accidental death being that of a woman who had administered to herself a large amount of cocaine in 1927. By that time the ratification of the Geneva Convention had given rise to a black market in the distribution of adulterated drugs. In fact, the new policies—state control over importation and sale—produced in Europe a result very similar to that in effect in the United States a decade earlier. The smuggling of opium and cocaine, for example, quadrupled in Spain between 1924 and 1928.

The next international development was to be the 1931 convention, which took place in Geneva as well. This treaty must be considered the first victory of the prohibitionist spirit, since it not only established the so-called evaluations, or annual production quotas to be set by each country for legal uses, but in addition charged the Central Permanent Committee to "fight against addiction," laying the groundwork for a complex superstructure of international bodies that sheltered numberless officials. Penal regulations arrived five years later with the Geneva Treaty of 1936, the fruit of a conference organized and supervised by H. S. Ansliger. The text of that agreement urged all countries to create "specialized police services" and commited them to "severely punish, with prison sentences" not only illicit traffic, but possession as well.

At least nominally, the American crusade had become a world crusade. Culminating without public alarms, almost muted, this change passed by almost unperceived by European doctors. Proof of this is Louis Lewin's *Phantastica,* a fundamental treatise of modern psychopharmacology, published in 1927, which did not even report the change. Referring with irony to the dry laws, and ignoring that the antialcohol prohibition was rapidly being extended to other pharmaceuticals, he says:

> Why this excessive effort only against alcohol? Why is there not also a general crusade against morphine, heroin, cocaine, nicotine, love, and gambling? The fight against alcohol is not based on clear judgments, but on prejudices. When there is no delinquent act other than excess in drinking, my advice is to consider that excess as a strictly private affair. It causes as little harm to others as the voluntary taking of morphine or cocaine, or the intoxication by caffeine by taking too much coffee. Every man has the right to harm himself, and it is incorrect to limit that right except if he were to be enlisted in the military.

But undeniably an effort was present to eliminate from the surface of the Earth all derivatives of the poppy and of coca, ignoring the right mentioned by Lewin. Furthermore, what began in 1936 with four substances was to be extended to dozens of others, old and new.

CHAPTER THIRTEEN

New Drugs

An extraordinary discovery, commercialized during the thirties, was that of certain amines (amphetamine, dexamphetamine, methamphetamine), which appeared as products freely sold in pharmacies for nasal congestion, dizziness, obesity, depression, and the treatment of sedative overdoses. They were really stimulants of the nervous system, ten or twenty times more active than cocaine, much cheaper, and capable of not only improving endurance but of considerably improving scores in certain tests such as the intelligence quotient (IQ).

Their powerful euphoric effect led to their being sold to treat all discomforts related to depression, and they were given in sometimes formidable amounts to soldiers in World War II. They would reduce appetite sometimes for days, as well as sleep, nausea, exhaustion, and discouragement—something too tempting for military hierarchies, which began using them in the Spanish Civil War and launched full methamphetamine use with highly stressed troops from 1939 to 1945. The Germans, British, Italians, and Japanese, especially, distributed hundreds of millions of annual doses as a supplement to war rations, even though plenty of lethal intoxications occurred. Japan, for example, increased the production of this stimulant to the maximum during the war.

Upon surrender, the warehoused excess disappeared, producing a flooding of the streets with those drugs, which in 1950 supplied one million delirious users and several other million who were less suicidal, the perpetrators of over half of the murders and self-inflicted permanent cerebral lesions, and being admitted by the hundreds into hospitals, with a diagnosis of furious schizophrenia. In England, the greater part of amphetamines ended up in Montgomery's army and the Royal Air Force, and in 1941 a newspaper from the capital carried the headline "Methedrine Wins the Battle of London."

The postwar period modified user patterns, shifting the use of these amines to older persons, housewives, and students: groups subject to boredom and lack of motivation or to the stress of having to face examinations. The free-sales regime alternated with advertisements such as "Two pills are better than one month's vacation," and soon there were moderate and immoderate users all over the planet. In 1950 the United States produced about one thousand tons yearly—eighty doses per capita, children included—a rate equaled by other nations. Amphetamine and dexamphetamine inhalers were considered medicines comparable to menthol lozenges and soothing ointments, and their use in sports led to doping. Toward the end of the fifties, a world champion cyclist died during an ascent aided by Maxiton, a methamphetamine. Shortly thereafter, twenty-three participants of the European Tour fell sick upon leaving Luchon, with symptoms described by the race doctor as caused by acute amphetamine intoxication. Two rounds later, a newspaper related that "it was necessary to put one of the contestants in a straight jacket because he suffered an insanity crisis" after ingesting one hundred pills of Tenedron, another amphetamine.

Apart from that, the landscape of secondary side effects had been known since the end of the thirties. Autopsies performed on adolescent addicts showed a visceral deterioration equivalent to that of old people, clearly showing the price paid for "speed." Toxic psychosis or death can result from doses of less than one-tenth of a gram, and chronic use produces insomnia, loss of appetite, and aggressive excitability, if not a permanent persecution mania. In comparison with cocaine, they give rise to greater tolerance (the need to increase the dose to retain the same effect), and they metabolize much more slowly, increasing the risk of acute intoxication. But they were commercialized originally in the United States, and until the seventies, no American delegation supported their international control. This can be understood when it is considered that they are synthetic products, exported to developing countries instead of the other way around, with patents underlying their commercialization. Their use was also encouraged by the fact that users included a wide spectrum of professions, not particularly identified with low-income or marginal groups; this avoided the generation of stigma mechanisms based on racial and social prejudices.

The discovery of amphetamines was followed by that of other high-powered stimulants, beginning with phenmetracine (introduced to Spain as Preludin, among other names), which became enormously popular until the mid-seventies. Apart from Japan and Germany, especially afflicted by World War II, the existence of such drugs in Europe and the United States produced cases of excessive use among adults, although these were small compared with the number of cases of moderate or occasional use. What attracted the most attention were gangs of adolescents injecting themselves intravenously with large amounts of speed, although surprisingly, that occurred mainly in Sweden and North America, pioneers in prohibiting free sale. Spain, because of its long-standing tolerance, became the dispenser to Europe and eventually to the world. It did not register a single case of adolescent addiction to amphetamines, although in 1969—by which time the use of these substances had a twenty-year history there—a survey among students showed that 66 percent of them had used or were using them.

This information needs to be put in the context that this consumption was often recommended by the family doctor at the time of examinations, and enjoyed the approval of parents, avoiding the glamour of the forbidden to the proverbially rebellious age of youth. Consequently, no black market existed, in contrast with the situation in less permissive countries. Although consumption was not limited to study or work situations, and recreational use rose at certain festive times of the year, most consumers exercised satisfactory self-control.

Barbiturates enjoyed a popularity comparable to that of the stimulants. If the word *narcotic* is taken literally—as something that produces numbness in the user—one could say that barbiturates, among known drugs, are the ones with the highest capacity to produce numbness, were it not for the appearance in the end of the fifties of the neuroleptics, or major tranquilizers: compounds able to compete with barbiturates for that dubious honor. But numbness became useful, especially in the absence of opiates—more so if alcohol was banned, as was the case in North America when massive sales of them started. Contrary to stimulants, barbiturates incline to extroversion and disinhibition; their effect is to produce a state between alcoholic inebriation and sleep, providing numbness as a release for those pursued by their conscience, and satisfaction obtained by the timid when they are able to access their nerve. We must add to those qualities the almost inevitable ability to kill in high doses: a detail that converted these drugs into the most common means of committing suicide.

But the fact that they were not "narcotics" under the law, and their free sales without prescription throughout the world, with an honorable description as "sedatives, not opiates," led many people to have a container of barbiturates in their night tables, with foreseeable results. By 1965 about 135,000 British subjects were dependent on these drugs, and in Scandinavia, by 1960, 73 percent of addicts were users of barbiturates. In 1962 a doctor stated before a special committee created by President Kennedy that there might be 250,000 American addicts ("and they are addicts who ignore their status," he added)—not an inflated number, considering that by then the nation manufactured some thirty tablets per capita annually. In narcotic power, this production was equivalent to four thousand tons of crude opium, and we must remember that the first voices of alarm on account of the "narcotic problem" were raised in the Unites States when imports amounted to two hundred tons annually.

Otherwise, any competent doctor had known since the twenties that there is no worse dependency that is more destructive to personality. Studies made within the American prison population from 1945 to 1948 showed that "the same convicts subjected to doses of morphine and heroin were sensate, prudent, able, and scarcely affected sexually, while under the effects of barbiturates they became obstinate, aggressive, capable of masturbation in public, repeating idle excuses for their stumbling gait and mumbling speech." The catastrophic withdrawal syndromes were also well known, much more prolonged than that of heroin and with greater risks of death, both in the convulsive phase and in the later protracted delirium. Last, there existed the possibilities of accidental overdose; this occurred when people ingested pills when inebriated, or else took some, forgot they had done so, and took them again, as probably happened to Marilyn Monroe.

There was no other legal recourse regarding "functional disturbances and insomnia," one of the main reasons to visit a doctor until different hypnotics and sedatives were introduced, and combinations of barbiturates and amphetamines were the rage in medical offices, since they avoided extensive testing of patients. Despite their ability to serve as a comfortable remedy for "nerves"—available, inexpensive, and pure—during the space of almost fifty years, only some few million people became addicted to these drugs and had to travel that miserable road. The great majority had the same bottle of Veronal or Luminal in their night tables for months or years and used it with moderation. As was the case with stimulant amines, barbiturates were never linked to social or ethnic minorities, and the absence of stigma protected them from the passion for the forbidden.

Among the drugs discovered during the period between the two world wars, we must mention several dozen synthetic opiates. The preparations for a second world conflict induced armies to search for anesthetics that were independent of the poppy, synthethized from coal tar and heavy oils, and they were introduced around 1945.

One of the common ones was pethidine, commercialized as Dolantin by Hoechst, and introduced as a nonaddictive analgesic. In 1952 some five hundred people addicted to the drug were admitted to American hospitals, unable to suppress a habit induced by their own doctors in 81 percent of the cases. By 1967 the American production of pethidine reached nineteen tons, sold under more than eighty different names.

Methadone turned out to be seven times more active; it was discovered by German army chemists and originally christened Dolofin by Adolf Hitler, although it was considered to be too addictive and toxic, and was never given to German troops. In 1964, under several names, some ten tons were consumed in the United States. Ketobemidone was similar to methadone, although nine times more active, and even by 1963 hundreds of kilograms were still being manufactured in Europe after the drug had already been classified as "extradangerous." Dextromoramide (Palfium), a euphoric agent at least three times more active than heroin, also received popular acclaim; it was introduced as a "manageable, powerful, and nonaddictive pharmaceutical." Similar descriptions would be applied to normethadone, morphinone, dihydro-morphinone, and a list of more than seventy other narcotics by 1960.

Their history was the same: they were first marketed as drugs without the disadvantages observed in others, later their addictive capacity became evident, and after a few years they fell under the restricted category. Any substance with an anesthetic power equal or superior to that of heroin can give rise to addiction if frequently used. The scandal attached to synthetic narcotics did not focus on the long period during which they were freely available but on the pretense that a nonopiate tranquilizer would be a harmless tranquilizer. Prohibition of the natural opiates incited this picaresque pharmacology.

But the success of synthetic narcotics amounted to nothing compared with that of other drugs introduced during the fifties. Described as remedies for "the rhythm of modern life," their effect in small and medium doses is that of muscle relaxants, which instead of producing the emotional analgesia of opium (with its rich currents of dreamlike visions) give rise to an intellectual analgesia, characterized by logic and esthetic indifference.

Meprobamate, another petroleum derivative, was introduced in 1955 under hundreds of different names, with an unprecedented publicity barrage, as a "happy pill, granting moral tranquillity without addiction," even though three years later several experiments showed that its spectacular withdrawal syndrome closely resembled that of alcohol/barbiturates. Nevertheless, six hundred tons of this drug were consumed in the United States in 1965, and several thousand in the rest of the world; in that same year, for example, India notified the United Nations that this "happy pill" was creating many cases of imbecility and dependence among the middle and upper classes of that country, who lined up behind the cause of substituting traditional opium for scientific medicines.

The kilos of meprobamate were soon to be exceeded—and later tripled—by the benzodiazepines, which arrived as anxiolytics ("dissolvers of anxiety") and hypnotics, free of addictive properties. Studies published in 1961 showed that the withdrawal syndrome of the benzodiazepines (Valium, diazepam, Aneural, Orfidal, Rohypnol, Dormodor, etc.) included trembling, nausea, muscular fibrillation, anorexia, insomnia, depression, and convulsive crises lasting several days.

Several thousand tons of many other hypnotics and sedatives were sold. The one with the bitterest memory was softenon, or thalidomide, commercialized in 1957 as a "harmless sleeping pill, ideal for pregnant women." Two years later, the birth of deformed babies began, rising to more than three thousand and producing a wave of abortions in Europe as well as a famous euthanasia trial in Liege, where one doctor and four relatives were absolved.

Among the novelties of the period was the diethylamide of lysergic acid, or LSD 25, a semisynthetic drug, extracted from the ergot fungus, discovered by Albert Hofmann in 1943. This was an extraordinary substance, dosed in millionths, not hundredths or thousandths of a gram, as those known until then were. Its therapeutic margin (the ratio between active and lethal doses) was practically unlimited, and its tolerance was negligible because its effect ceased when it was used daily, regardless of the amounts consumed. It was a pharmaceutical manufactured at minimal cost (one dose costing one cent), starting from a fungus ubiquitous in grain cultivating zones, which when used in amounts almost invisible to the human eye would create "an experience of unimaginable intensity."

Fully understanding the variety of uses that such a substance might be put to, Hofmann conceived a preparation—Delysid—which Sandoz was to give to psychotherapists throughout the world, with notable success if we take into consideration that the amount of material published by 1965 in scientific magazines about LSD 25 exceeded in diversity and extent what had been published about all other drugs discovered in the century. The greatest successes were secured in general psychotherapy, where it generated a percentage of intended or consummated suicides equal to or inferior to that applicable to other treatments; in deathbed therapy, where it performed better than other diverse narcotics in 30 to 80 percent of cases; and as a stimulus for alcoholics to abandon their addiction.

The Delysid prospectus rested on two basic effects of LSD: "to provoke liberation of repressed material in the patient, and to provide a mental relaxation" and to "induce short-term model psychosis in normal subjects." The latter was directed to the psychotherapist, since it was considered useful to generate "a deeper vision of the world of ideas and sensations in your patient," but it interested the American Office of Strategic Services (OSS), which had already used mescaline and hemp extracts to detect communist sympathizers within the armed forces. Funds and support for these activities depended upon a council headed by General W. Donovan, the president of the American Medical Association, Commissioner Ansliger, and Dr. H. Strughold, a German citizen accused of atrocities while working in the Dachau concentration camp. When the OSS became the CIA, its chemical division launched—as Project MK-ULTRA—a vast secret program of LSD research under the more general rubric "nonconventional war agents." The project included the creation of some foundations, and generous grants were given to several prominent North American psychiatrists; Dr. H. Abramson, for example, received $85,000 in 1953 to investigate whether LSD was "effective" in creating

> a. memory disturbances; b. discrediting due to aberrant behavior; c. alteration of sexual habits; d. handing over of information; e. suggestibility; f. dependency.

Guided by the general objective of launching "surprise attacks" against "anti-American" elements, the research continued until 1960, when it became apparent that many researchers working on project MK-ULTRA were themselves taking the drug recreationally, and other psychiatrists involved agreed with Abramson that

> the effect is an essentially joyous disturbance of the ego function. . . . Users generally enjoy the experience.

Something considered to produce insanity in normal persons in 1953 had by 1959 been transformed into a euphoria-causing agent, useful for purposes of introspection and creativity. Under those circumstances, it became not only useless but dangerous for interests represented by the CIA, which had been buying from Sandoz one million doses weekly, and already had formidable stocks of it.

These and other data were made public in 1977, prodded by a congressional subcommittee headed by Senator Kennedy. We now know that specialized sections of the marines, the army, and the CIA used, as uninformed test subjects, thousands of American soldiers and civilians, and an undetermined number—much higher—of Laotians, Cambodians, and Vietnamese. One of the few confirmed victims was Lieutenant F. Olson, who jumped out of a window several days after being given a punch loaded with LSD without his knowledge, while attending a work-related meeting with other CIA colleagues.

CHAPTER FOURTEEN

A Pharmacratic Peace

It was foreseeable that the appearance of so many active drugs implied a reinforcement of the "white" market and adversely affected the big smugglers and sellers of alcohol during Prohibition, who placed their hopes in transferring their business from wines and liquors to cocaine and heroin. An illegal cocaine had no future, forced to compete with the legal stimulant amines, so they could anticipate business only if it involved natural opiates.

In 1934, when alcohol prohibition was ended, a syndicate now without internal disputes, although very impoverished, maintained traditional control over prostitution and aimed to consolidate its position in gambling, trusting that the prohibition of heroin would allow it sooner or later to put a new emporium in place. The "families" mutually agreed to distribute "zones of influence" between themselves, and the interior secretary of that underground government was Salvatore "Lucky" Luciano, confidence man of Genovese, while the Department of the Treasury post was held by Meyer Lansky, confidence man of Aaron Rothstein and the Jewish branch. To ensure an immediate supply, with growth potentials, Luciano and Lansky traveled to Asia Minor and the Far East in 1935, the former contacting secret societies in Shanghai, allied with Chiang Kai-shek in the civil wars, while the latter established dialogues with Turkish and Lebanese opium producers and somewhat later with the Corsican Mafia in Marseilles to install refineries in their zone of influence.

Supplies lasted well into 1939, when the modest but promising heroin business was threatened by World War II. This led to Lansky's journeys to Mexico to establish poppy plantations, and to Cuba, where it is said he made contact with Bayer representatives, transported by German submarines. The situation became critical, nevertheless, because Luciano had been convicted, practically for life (under a prostitution charge, not for heroin trafficking), Genovese was also behind bars, and the connection with the Germans through Cuba was nothing but a bomb waiting to explode. It was then that Luciano's lawyer, M. Polakoff—previously a high-ranking police official, as well as a federal district attorney—presented to his client a certain offer made by the Secret Service. The offer was a pardon to be granted to Luciano and Genovese, provided their syndicate collaborated with the Allied invasion of Sicily (in exchange for exclusivity in delivering supplies in Italy) and with the boycott of German submarines, which operated with relative freedom—perhaps provided with fuel by that same syndicate—off the Atlantic coast of North America. Luciano returned to Sicily, soon to die, and the now almighty Lansky not only accepted the resignation of Polakoff but also his advice that his perfect substitute be the young Richard S. Nixon, an active attorney who would rise through several other assignments until he became president of his country.

At the end of the war, in 1945, neither the French nor the Asian connections had been reestablished, and the price of heroin was seventy times higher in the United States than it was in 1939. But the CIA was soon to make two decisions that would revitalize those connections. The first was to support the Corsican gangsters in taking over dock facilities in the south of France, to edge out the socialist and communist syndicates. The second was to protect anticommunist troops hiding in the Golden Triangle, believing that they might serve as a bulwark against Mao and even might reconquer China. This support was manifested through two airlines (Civil Air Transport, based in Taiwan, and Sea Supply Corporation, based in Bangkok) whose airplanes would deliver arms and munitions to the guerrillas and would return—admittedly—with tons of opium. Even in 1954, when the United States decided to assume the difficult inheritance of Vietnam from the French, the CIA again decisively cooperated in a connection between the Golden Triangle and Saigon, where a dozen gangsters from Corsica and Marseilles arrived as "logistical support" for the local hierarchy to smooth out the obstacles against the exportation of heroin sponsored by Ngo Dinh Nhu, brother to President Diem, among others. In Thailand also, where a good part of the opium from the Golden Triangle was refined, the supply was maintained thanks to General Phao, supreme chief of police, described in a CIA memo as "loyal ally, ever ready to use force against any leftist temptation of the government."

It is evident then, that in the famous "connections" there was a close involvement between the enforcers and the violators of the law from the very beginning. Luciano had to negotiate in Shanghai with the Reds or with the Greens, Chinese crime syndicates linked with the British or French Secret Services, respectively. Lansky installed his refineries in Beirut and Marseilles with the approval of the Office of Strategic Services, and the Mafia multiplied its strength in Italy thanks to the American Secret Service. In order to pay for anticommunist loyalties, the CIA collaborated decisively in the first massive shipments of opium and heroin from Southeast Asia. Among all of the coincidences we include the fact that high officials of police and justice departments, such as Polakoff—not to mention Nixon himself—began or ended their careers by serving as counsels to Lansky.

All of these actions took place *before* any increase in the number of heroin addicts or simply before users of the drug were detected in the United States. In 1956, for example, the prison population of users had not yet reached one thousand; half of them were blacks, Puerto Ricans, and Mexicans. Pushed by repressive measures, the traditional user—white, older than forty, employed, and well off—had already moved on to consume synthetic legal opiates (such as methadone) or barbiturates and alcohol. The new type of user, with a median age of twenty-five, usually belonged to more delinquent or less decorous environments, stood up as not generally employable, and was rarely blond. Something was happening similar to what was predicted by the first prohibitionist crusaders: opium and its derivatives were drugs used by "puerile and degenerate races." On the other hand, those "degenerates" were few in number and had no appeal to the rest of society. Adding both, the "drug problem" seemed about to be resolved.

Nevertheless, in order for that to happen, it was necessary that (1) the small black market not be stimulated, especially by laws that would increase its margin of profit; and (2) the addict not become an esthetic-literary-social figure, with paradoxical, although clear, side benefits. But in 1951, urged by Anslinger, Congress approved the Boggs Act, which imposed minimum two-year sentences for a "first offense," meaning the possession of any amount, expressly forbidding appeal or parole. If the Harrison Act had deprived the medical establishment of the power of decision over what constituted the "medical use" of certain drugs, the Boggs law stripped judges of the authority to decide what constituted a just and appropriate sentence. Now the whole matter became a police affair from beginning to end, and the American Bar Association, the professional association of attorneys, asked Congress to revise the precept, understanding it to be injurious to fundamental judicial principles.

Afraid of a debate on the constitutionality of the law, the legislative branch decided to name a subcommittee under Senator Daniels, which would deliberate for the next four years. Called to testify as an expert, Anslinger declared in 1954 that a "serious drug problem" continued to exist, and he denounced a communist plot based on the illicit exportation of opiates from the Mediterranean and Southeast Asia to North America. His department, the FBN (Federal Bureau of Narcotics), later to become the DEA (Drug Enforcement Administration), needed to increase the number of agents or else lose a crucial battle.

We will never know to what degree Anslinger knew the

heroin business had been installed with the direct or indirect support of the CIA and other American governmental agencies. In any case, the result of his testifying was a spectacular increase in employees—from three hundred to three thousand, later to become ten thousand—and a report of the Daniels subcommittee against any "permissiveness" in view of an evident Russian-Chinese maneuver to demoralize America. From that report, a new law was to emerge: the Narcotics Control Act of 1956, which raised the penalty for the first offense to five years in prison and empowered juries to impose the death penalty on anyone over eighteen who sold heroin to a minor. The judges were still deprived of their capacity to tailor the sentence to each case, and the powers of federal agencies were increased to the maximum.

A minor, acting as a police informant or decoy, could ask for and obtain heroin from a seller, and could then send the latter to the electric chair or the gas chamber without having to prove damage done to him or to third parties. Although similar behaviors had since Roman times been considered typical cases of impossible crimes (such as killing a corpse), the impossible crime of selling illicit drugs to those who in principle should destroy it, the narcotics police, was equated to the crime of poisoning specific persons without their consent. The simple intention was enough; the cases included those where the intention might have been influenced by a deliberate plan to provoke it (the entrapment of doctors and pharmacists, for example) and could not for that reason be considered spontaneous.

Shortly after the new law was enacted in 1957, the black market prospered with increasing prices and was using "camels": minors involved in street trafficking. The famous Appalachian meeting took place that same year, when the syndicate decided to abandon small-scale operations and risk a policy of massive imports, using Havana as an intermediate stop.

To complete the picture, along with the draconian legal measures, the junkie appeared—a personage previously unknown, blending qualities of the martyr as well as those of a follower of Count Dracula and acting out the dismemberment of life in extreme consumer societies: some accepted postponing their enjoyments to secure them by means of labor, while others wanted them cheaply and immediately, impatient and indifferent to the expenditure of any effort. For the latter, the means of obtaining their wishes was to reduce them all to a single ritual, repeated endlessly in minute detail, defined by the oldest of the "official" junkies, the writer William Burroughs, as "the algebra of need." One must secure injectable heroin, consume it as fast as possible, and restart the cycle; the world is reduced to that.

The new addict was obliged to sell in order to consume, exposing himself to penalties of prison for life, or even death—not to mention poisoning by substitutes or adulterated merchandise. But he carried an emptiness in the center of his being, which made anything seem better than the absence of an effective narcotic, and found in his circle of peers an identity as masochistic as it was simple, with an overwhelming indifference that, above all, bestowed the feeling of not owing anything to anyone. A Burroughs reader, converted to the club of the irresponsible, described it thus:

> Of course I would like to lead a decent life. We all would. But I am hooked, I cannot escape. I cannot clean up and earn a living, and wake up and prepare breakfast, and pay taxes. I need my injections.

Those addicted to opium and its derivatives generally used them as sources of energy, to comply with duties (domestic or professional) that would prove arduous without those anesthetics. Now, however, the addict sought the opposite: even when he took ten or twenty times less the amount than his predecessors, he did so declaring himself generally irresponsible, instead of better assuming his responsibilities. The old addict and the new junkie coincided in an internal lack of hospitality, mitigated by heroin. But the different routes of access reversed the terms. Although euphoria was the aim for both, in one case it created marginalization, and in the other social integration; in one case it led to crimes justified on the basis of need and risk, and in the other to an effort to continue to function at the level of self and social expectations.

Beleaguered by severe legislation, but simultaneously compensated by the solution it entailed, the numbers of new heroin addicts quickly multiplied. In 1956, when the Narcotics Control Act was passed, the number of Americans imprisoned for heroin possession was less than one thousand. In 1960 the special prosecutor in charge of drug cases, M. Ambrose, declared that there were ten times more and that at least another fifty thousand were loose in the streets. As happened during Prohibition with the large alcohol distributors, not a single large distributor of heroin was captured or condemned for that reason; those in prison were retailers or small-scale resellers.

While this triple and interrelated phenomenon was happening—severe legal repression, a clear reinvigoration of the syndicate, and the emergence of the new addict—the pre–World War I spirit was reborn in the United States. The Loyalty Program, installed by President Truman in 1947, was designed to intern or imprison in concentration camps any "sympathizer with totalitarian ideas," and as an internal reflection of the Korean War (1950–1953), with the nation in a state of nationalist fervor, the ideological inquisitions were coordinated by Senator Joseph McCarthy, presiding over the famous Anti-American Activities committee; his right hand in the committee was an old counsel to Meyer Lansky, now the U.S. Representative Richard Nixon.

But along with a buoyant economy and the wave of patriotism, defenders of the left soon appeared, and even total dissidents, such as Burroughs himself, who saw the American dream as a fraud and a nightmare. Socially, this lack of satisfaction was manifested by diffuse and generalized rejection by the adolescent "rebels without a cause" and the "angry young men" who saw nonconformity as an ethical and esthetic alternative to the attitudes represented by national heroes such as McCarthy and Anslinger. In 1957 the term *hipster* was first used: "one is *hip* or *square*," said Norman Mailer, "a rebel or a square cell, entrapped in the totalitarian cloth of American society, forced to bend in order to succeed."

The work of the joint committee formed by the American Medical Association and the American Bar Association had begun two years before, enlarged by social scientists from several universities, to search for a viable alternative to the official policy on drug affairs. Their conclusions, published in a provisional report in 1958 and later as a book entitled *Drug Addiction: Crime or Disease* (Bloomington, Ind.: Indiana University Press, 1977), maintained that the crusade was a pseudomedical and extrajudicial enterprise that could only result in crime and marginalization. Based on the concept of the self-fulfilling prophecy, recently introduced by the sociologist R. K Merton, the pharmacological crusade presented a circular pattern, where a certain image of reality is imposed, and then exhibited as an effect independent of the imposition; that the users of certain drugs were adolescents, criminals, undesirables, or beggars was not to be attributed to some substance or other, but to the law itself.

The report included two appendices. The first lauded the British system of treating addicts—prescribing heroin or morphine at no cost or with a minimal charge—because of the practical results as well as its fundamental theoretical basis. The second criticized American legislation for omitting the formal and substantive requirements implicit in any positive regulation in a nation based on the principles of law.

Considering the civic and professional category of the editors, this document was without a doubt the greatest attack launched against prohibitionism, and it eventually forced Anslinger's resignation. Its echoes even reached Congress, where Senator S. Fiddle presented the junkie subculture as the "ideology of justification"; whether conditioned or not by societal factors, the psyche of those individuals inclined them to feel like impotent victims of a weak will and institutional persecution.

In view of the sudden turn of events, the administration had no recourse but to either enter into even greater conflict with the medical, judicial, and the so-called social science establish-

ments or yield in some areas. It was a matter of granting some
competencies (or more exactly, return them) to those establishments while attempting to keep enforcement prerogatives. It was
then that the new United States representative to the United Nations, Anslinger, accepted the new preamble of the convention,
signed in New York, which declares that the "medical use of narcotics will remain necessary to alleviate pain, and their availability
is to be guaranteed." This convention merged those of The Hague
and Geneva, adding new substances to the controlled list, but the
expressed declaration in the preamble dismantled prior patient
efforts by the American FNB to classify opium and its derivatives
as unnecessary or useless and to impose this criterion upon the
international community. Joining the renewal, the Supreme Court
ruled unanimously and importantly in 1962 that

> the addict is not free to control himself without help
> from the outside. If addicts were to be punished for
> their addiction, the insane would have to be punished
> for their insanity.

Things seemed to change dramatically in a short time. Traffic being forbidden but personal use allowed, the situation of the
user of illicit drugs seemed to be similar to that of the alcohol
user during Prohibition. Alcohol drinkers, however, did not
need to be "treated and rehabilitated," while the user of opiates, cocaine, and hemp turned out to be ill, and identical to a
sufferer from ulcers or pneumonia, except that the disease was
considered an epidemic, treatable by quarantine. Some scholars
immediately pointed out this incongruence, preceded by the
psychiatrist T. Szasz, who named the process "therapeutism."
He was followed shortly by H. Becker, who in that same year
published a general theory of deviation as a learned label entitled
Outsiders: Studies in the Sociology of Deviation (New York: Free
Press, 1963), establishing a technical means of measuring self-
fulfilling prophecies. The third dissident was the jurist E. Schur,
with his notion of "victimless crime"; the use of drugs was only

one among many other crimes without *corpus delicti,* such as homosexuality, pacifism, prostitution, euthanasia, gambling in nonauthorized locations, and pornography, where a "voluntary exchange, among adults, of highly solicited goods and services" takes place, instead of damage denounced by victims or others.

The voices of protest from moderate pharmacologists also increased. International regulation was subject to the Addictive Drugs Expert Committee—eight persons "enjoying universal respect and confidence because of their technical qualifications and their impartiality"—but a technical definition of *addictive drug* was missing. Finally, in 1953 the committee declared that those drugs "induced a joint addiction, tolerance, and physical dependence," but there was no way to include cocaine or hemp in that definition, or to exclude alcohol, barbiturates, and a long list of other substances. In view of the protests inspired by that declaration, the experts proposed to "actualize it" four years later in 1957, stating that prohibited drugs induced "addiction," and the permitted ones only induced "habit."

The difference was so far removed from pharmacology that it resembled the difference between dirty and clean, when in fact something closer to biology was expected from the committee. Many toxicologists were not satisfied, and one of the experts said: "Strange as it may seem, drug abuse has never received a clear scientific explanation." It was scandalous that after three decades of international regulation of narcotics, an even minimally acceptable definition of those substances was not to be found. Tired of attempting to define that which was prohibited, while already burdened with a list of prohibited substances, H. Halbach, chief of the division of pharmacology and toxicology of WHO (World Health Organization) and secretary of the Addictive Drug Expert Committee, simply stated that "it is impossible to establish a correlation between biological data and administrative regulations." For that same reason, the Expert Committee proposed the "substitution of the terms *addiction* and *habit* by *dependence*" and changed its name to Committee of Experts on Drugs that Create Dependence." Thus, the *pharmacological* distinction between licit and illicit drugs, medicines, and narcotics, disappeared. Prohibitionist legislation was not put in place by toxicologists, chemists, or even doctors, and WHO now—in 1963—clarified that legal measures could not be justified in scientific, biological terms. Although the expression "physical or psychical dependence" suffered from a disconcerting vagueness, there was no better way to describe the list of illegal drugs. Based in Geneva, within the WHO organization, the Committee of Experts also distanced itself from enforcement agencies—the Narcotics Bureau, the Narcotics Commission, and the International Board of Narcotics Control, based in Vienna—even to the point of disparaging the Viennese agencies themselves.

One can say, therefore, that by the beginning of the seventies, a critical dialogue about Prohibition was in full force. The moderate faction negated the distinction between narcotics and medicines, proposing to approach dependence on any drug as something coming from the individual, not from the drug. The radical faction went beyond that, wielding three related propositions: (1) "toxicomania," or addiction, received a stereotypical definition, which generated distortion; (2) no administration had the right to protect adults against themselves; (3) making certain drugs illegal was not only ineffective but in fact counterproductive in preventing abuse.

In the opposite corner, the interests and values that insisted on preserving the status quo remained intact. It was then that a medical orientation appeared to mediate between the critics and the old guard by proposing to consider the user of certain drugs as an ill person. Therapeutism had been discarded several decades before as incompatible with repression, but new life was injected into the idea that curing and repressing could complement each other, and this complementarity gave rise to a practically unlimited new gamut of experts and consultants. What Szasz named *pharmacracy,* a power based on monopolizing drugs desired by others, arose only when enforcement agencies and illicit traffic organizations were joined by this third component, which was moderately reformist and would begin to absorb ever increasing portions of the funds appropriated to prevent the use of certain drugs.

If anything characterized the first decades of the crusade, it was the "smallness" of the problem. In 1960, for example, conflicts remained local in the United States and minimal around the rest of the globe. A calculation of the numbers of civilized persons consuming opium, heroin, and hemp indicates that Prohibition was a success; compared with a population of hundreds of millions in Europe and America, the actual users were hardly 200,000—a ridiculously low figure.

But chemists and laboratories found and offered legal alternatives to the banned drugs, and their efforts supplied the pharmacies of the planet with an astonishing variety of drugs. In fact, the number of people who habitually used a pharmacy product multiplied eight- or tenfold, even though the majority of them was unaware of being dependent on a psychoactive compound. It was a time when official toxicologists, beginning with Anslinger, enjoyed full public confidence; they substituted one pharmacopoeia for another, with the criterion of preferring the synthetic over the natural, the patented over the unpatentable. In 1960 there were about forty-five thousand junkies in the United States, with another forty-five thousand cocaine and hemp users. But the total of semisynthetic and synthetic opiates, sedatives, barbiturates, hypnotics, and tranquilizers reached two thousand tons, with an activity comparable to that of twenty-thousand tons of opium. Since that was more than three times the maximum amount consumed in China at the end of the nineteenth century, North Americans seemed to be consuming some twelve times more narcotic substances than the Chinese ever did.

Let us consider stimulant use in the United States in the same year. Between amphetamines and phenmetracines, legal consumption reached some five hundred tons, equivalent to five thousand tons of cocaine; this implies a use about thirty times higher than in 1910. The consumption of caffeine—another stimulant and dependence-inducing alkaloid, present not only in edible liquids and solids but also in an enormous amount of pharmaceutical preparations—reached one-fourth of a kilo per capita per year. Under these very conditions, the United States embarked upon a campaign against the cultivation of coca, poppies, and hemp throughout the world. In 1961 the Department of Agriculture included tons of tobacco, excess from domestic demand, as part of its contribution to Food for Peace, the international program. The beer and spirits distilling associations had for decades financed Hollywood films, to make sure that someone offered a drink in all possible scenes—a mark of distinction in deluxe surroundings, or else a sign of cordial exchange in more modest environments. The tobacco manufacturers paid as well to have celluloid heroes and heroines shown always with a cigarette in their hands or mouths.

CHAPTER FIFTEEN

The Psychedelic Rebellion

In Europe and North America the most sought-after drugs had been stimulants and tranquilizers. The visionary drugs had hardly aroused any interest since the times of the Club des Haschischiens founded by Baudelaire and his friends. The poet Yeats and the play-wright O'Neill had briefly commented on their encounters with peyote early in the twentieth century. But shortly thereafter, a lively interest in this type of substance as a vehicle of knowledge was generated, started by Walter Benjamin and Aldous Huxley, soon to be joined by Ernst Junger, Robert Graves, Antonin Artaud, Henri Michaux, and R. G Wasson. Their experiences were at first isolated and never in accord; what was common among them ended up provoking something as unexpected as a movement of active op-position to prohibitionism. For the first time in its long history, the explicit use of certain drugs became linked to "a conspiracy of high politics" (Nietzsche), producing a discourse intended to affect the philosophy of its time. When those theses took root in the youth, they were to be considered the most dangerous plague of insanity registered in the annals of human history.

To ignore the Sandoz group for the moment, the first to mean-ingfully journey with LSD was a curious individual by the name of A. Hubbard, whose tireless advocacy of it allowed thousands of people to try it. After humble beginnings in the Prohibition Bureau during the dry law period, he began a flourishing career in the OSS, which would take him to high public offices and a job as a high executive in mining and uranium processing.

Nevertheless, "psychedelics" (from *psyche* and *delos:* mind enlargement) were to reach the greater public through the commentary of Aldous Huxley and his first experience with mescaline. *The Doors of Perception,* published shortly thereafter in 1954, proposed the need to go beyond the Platonic-Christian dualism (flesh and spirit, heaven and Earth, subject and object), with its fundamental incoherence revealed in great clarity by means of visionary trances. A similar proposal, although in a more cryptic tone, had been already developed by Ernst Junger in *Visit to Godenholm* (1952), remembering experiences with LSD held with Albert Hofmann. Junger's book received scant attention, while Huxley's caused a sensation; according to a contemporary chronicle:

> An apology for mescaline would be considered idiotic and worthless, but the matter deserves a more careful review, since we are dealing with one of the masters of English prose, a man of fabulous education, who usually exhibits a very high moral seriousness.

Thanks to A. Hubbard—whom he referred to as "our representative before the Supreme Powers"—Huxley soon extended his experimentation to LSD and psilocybin. The results so astonished him that he devoted the remaining nine years of his life to reflect upon them. Those nine years were also the duration of the MK-ULTRA project of the CIA, with diametrically opposite aims but using the same pharmaceuticals. Both were searching for "truth drugs," and these substances hardly went along with furtiveness. In *Heaven and Hell* (1956), Huxley stated:

> I suspect these drugs are destined to play a role in human affairs at least as important as that of alcohol up to now, and an incomparably more beneficial one. . . .

> One can really know, by experience, the meaning of
> "God is love," feeling that—in spite of death and suf-
> fering—everything is, in some way and in the final
> instance, perfectly all right.

A proposition such as this would "present problems without precedent to ministers of the world's organized religions," provoking "daily mysticisms." But Huxley believed that druggists sold filth for the multinationals, and the ramifications of this were extended to the agencies in charge of caring for world health, resulting essentially in an "aggression to human beings." More toxic and addictive than illicit drugs, the principal legal drugs had the added inconvenience of leading to conformism and brutalization, when in fact the challenge of the age was to

> find a way to allow the flowering of spontaneity and
> preservation of freedom, while at the same time letting
> technology develop to its desirable limits. It is an in-
> credibly complex problem, and also an immeasurably
> urgent one. . . . Now the human being is subjugated
> by what it has created, and bent to its laws, which are
> by no means humane laws.

When he wrote this in 1959, his ideas had taken root more or less firmly in some parts of Princeton, Chicago, Harvard, Yale, Berkeley, and other North American universities, feeding the image of a "counterculture" movement. Thinkers like Norman O. Brown and Herbert Marcuse were about to join the political debate, and the circle of literary and artistic people who surround Huxley continued to increase, no less than his general audience. The Cuban missile crisis was still recent and the United States sent the first battalions to Vietnam, not suspecting the coming slaughter there. Huxley was suffering from throat cancer and knew he would soon die, but he wrote more articles and made more public appearances. In "Culture and the Individual," his last publication, which appeared in *Playboy,* a magazine with a huge circulation at that time, he proposed the use of LSD and psilocybin to "discover new sources of energy" to overcome social and psychological inertia:

> With their help—as well as that of rigorous intellectual discipline—the individual could selectively adapt to his culture, reject the undesirable, the stupid, and the senseless, while accepting with gratitude the treasures of accumulated knowledge, rationality, compassion, and practical wisdom. If their numbers are sufficiently high, and their quality sufficiently polished, they might pass from selective adaptation to culture, to actual change and selective reform.

Consistent with his beliefs, Huxley—who had not taken visionary drugs for two years—asked to receive them as terminal therapy, and died peacefully while under the effects of two successive doses of LSD. The date was November 22, 1963, the same day on which President Kennedy was assassinated.

The circulation of this substance was legally permitted at that time, and the dossiers of psychiatrists and psychologists documented the treatment of some 35,000 Americans with it, among them Mrs. Robert Kennedy and Cary Grant. After seventy doses of LSD, Grant stated to the press that he was "reborn." In support therapy, or simply as experimental doses, California and especially Hollywood consumed a good part of the total consumption in the United States.

The first police actions date back to 1959 and mention small communities on the West Coast—specifically Seattle and Portland—where LSD was consumed in a manner similar to peyote in the Native American Church. According to the reports, "the participants do not belong to the American Indian race, and this gives rise to an understandable concern and protests" from farmers and social clubs. But these reports were filed, and there was no official concern until psychologist Timothy Leary launched the Psilocybin Project from the Personality Research Center of Harvard

University, the most prestigious university in the country.

The first experiment consisted of administering psilocybin to 175 healthy persons with diverse occupations, with a median age of thirty years. More than half of the subjects felt "permanently enriched" as a result of the tests, and 90 percent wanted to repeat them. Other experiments followed, including one with thirty-four prison inmates—murderers and muggers—who began to talk about love, ecstasy, and generosity of spirit. One year later, among Leary's experimental subjects, four categories could be identified: (1) students and alumni of Harvard, (2) teachers from Harvard and other universities, (3) a group of writers and artists, generally connected with the beat movement, and (4) celebrities or high-income individuals.

It didn't take long for Harvard to get alarmed; inventories of the substance were put under control, and further experiments were subjected to the approval of a committee. Nevertheless, one gram of LSD—ten thousand average doses—suddenly appeared from nonacademic sources, and the change in supply implied a change of attitude as well; while the psilocybin experience had been centered on love and caring, it now became based on death and resurrection. "We had produced some pagan magic," Leary commented much later, "putting in the balance our faith in human nature and the experience with these drugs."

Another year went by until the spring of 1963, when academic authorities aborted the project. Leary's termination, and that of his associates (psychologists R. Metzner and R. Alpert), happened when they dared to suspend medical supervision in some tests and to give psilocybin to a certain theologian to conduct experiments in a church. They had administered a total of some three thousand doses of psilocybin to four hundred persons, and still had plenty of LSD left. The situation demanded prudence, following the express advice of Huxley in the sense of maintaining the strictest scientific model possible. "I very strongly advise you," he wrote to Leary, "that nothing be done to involve sexuality, since we have enough problems as it is by suggesting that these drugs can produce esthetic and religious experiences."

But Leary in some ways was a Casanova—on top of being a man of some talent, lots of audacity, and an overwhelming charm —and the matter was no longer totally in his hands. Although he might have been more conciliatory and continued his experiments within a university framework for some time, the support of influential persons encouraged him to continue his research without hindrances. The heiress Peggy Mellon gave him a luxurious and well-supplied rural mansion in Millbrook, New York, as a base for continued operations, and the *Psychedelic Review* was available to spread his ideas. He could even boast that his connections reached the White House, because the rich and beautiful heiress Mary Pinchot, an initiate into visionary experience, was J. Kennedy's lover, and she probably gave Kennedy LSD at least once.

With *The Politics of Ecstasy* (1964), Leary popularly introduced Huxley's theses while advocating environmental issues ("We are ecology" was his primary motto) and an alternative to puritanism in general:

> Thanks to LSD, every human being could understand that the complete history of evolution is inscribed in his own body; every human being must recapitulate and discover the avatars of this central and majestic solitude.... The more time and attention are devoted to these explorations, the less men will be attached to vulgar pastimes. And this could be the solution to the problem of idleness.

Leary's discourse, with elements of science fiction and orientalism in it, gained special value because his book was published in the same year as Herbert Marcuse's *The One-Dimensional Man* and connected smoothly with that programmatic presentation of the American New Left. A hint of this is expressed in 1965 by C. Oglesby, leader of the main student organization in the nation:

The LSD experience marks one of life's boundaries, comparable to that of declaring adherence to a posture of radical politics. We took that step as a means of survival, as a healthy strategy.

These were times of growing opposition to the Vietnam War, combined with civil rights issues for blacks, student unrest, and terrorist groups such as the Weathermen—a sort of Anglo-Saxon "tupamarus" [a terrorist Peruvian group] capable of detonating several thousand bombs a year. Educated middle classes joined students and psychedelic communes to demand the legalization of marijuana consumption. In 1965, upon returning from a trip to Mexico, Leary was accused of possessing a few grams of hemp carried by his daughter at the border, and was quickly condemned to thirty years in prison. This sentence was eventually annulled by the Supreme Court with a not-guilty ruling not seen since the twenties. But while Leary appealed, a sheriff in California found one kilo of marijuana in his car, the court convicted him and he was sentenced—again very quickly—to ten years in jail. While in jail, he declared—also to *Playboy*—that the evident secret of LSD was its erotic potential, since a woman could have innumerable orgasms with a satisfactory experience with that drug. The Texas court that had sentenced him to thirty years then decided to retry him as top boss of the marijuana trade, asking for a life sentence, and the exprofessor came to play martyr of the system to a part of the country. It is difficult to believe, of course, that someone appealing a sentence as severe as a thirty-year one would dare carry one kilo of marijuana in his car. Leary always maintained that he was victim of a trap, but either the police were going to be convicted for fraud and conspiracy to frame a citizen, or he himself was to be convicted; suspecting the possible turn of events, he decided to escape, with the help of the Weathermen and other groups. He surfaced in Algeria as a political refugee, together with the leader of the Black Panthers, from there he went to Switzerland and ended up in Afghanistan, where he was turned over to the FBI and returned to prison. He languished there for quite a few years.

Meanwhile, the rebel contingent had increased in size, in part because the writer and activist Ken Kesey, originator of the type of psychedelic feast—with costumes, dances, strobe light effects, and rock music—that was later to become the typical discotheque. Kesey's activities crystallized in a series of festivals that culminated at Woodstock, where the hipster identity was reaffirmed. In 1970 the American administration estimated that some twenty-six million citizens consumed or had consumed marijuana, and eight million LSD.

The black market for this drug started in 1967, when it was first prohibited, promising to be very special. Contrary to its predecessors as illegal drugs, LSD did not require cultivation, was active in doses of millionths of a gram, and was a drug that advanced students as well as chemistry professors could synthesize to "feed the tribe." Police soon confiscated large stocks—some hundred million doses (ten kilos) appeared at the beginning of 1967, in a truck that was really a mobile laboratory—but the enforcement organization was opposed by the organization of the repressed. The principal producer group was the Brotherhood of Eternal Love, an association importing tons of marijuana and hashish from South America and Asia and using the profits from its sale to manufacture LSD and distribute it at low price, both in the United States and in Vietnam, as "a charitable distribution of a sacrament." The Brotherhood was founded, with all the formalities required of a charitable institution, ten days after LSD was made illegal in California. Its social objective was "to bring to the world a greater awareness of the divine, in the light of the sacred right of every individual to commune with God in spirit and in truth, as empirically revealed."

At the beginning of the seventies the high command of the Brotherhood (except for its leader J. Griggs, mysteriously poisoned shortly before) was convicted and severely sentenced, while the court expounded that "a pretty name will not hide objectives based on the degradation of the human race." The prosecution maintained that at its zenith, the organization consisted of some seven hundred and fifty persons, scattered over the five continents, and that the marijuana, hashish, and LSD traffic produced some $200 million for the "hippie Mafia."

Otherwise, the usual connection between this traffic and secret services became apparent. When ergotamine—a precursor to the synthesis of LSD—became scarce, the person who sold kilos of this drug to the Brotherhood was a certain "R. H. Stark," an alleged California hippie. Stark eventually turned out to be Khoury Ali, a Palestinian infiltrated by the CIA into international terrorist organizations. Contrary to other large traffickers of LSD, Stark/Ali was never processed by American justice, and even when Holland repatriated him in 1982 after capturing him with suitcases full of kilos of cocaine and heroin, he freely moved around California, although he soon died, without autopsy. It is difficult not to suspect that the hundreds of millions of doses sold by this intermediary—of a product considered "impeccable" by the Brother-hood's chemists—really came from the huge stock accumulated for years by the CIA in its program of "nonconventional war agents."

In May 1966 the redefinition of LSD and psilocybin as "drugs without any medical or scientific use" was submitted to a subcommittee of Congress, chaired by Senator Robert Kennedy. This redefinition was requested by two health representatives who were asked by Kennedy: "Why have they become drugs of no value, if they were of value six months ago?" Since no one could respond in medical-scientific terms, the brother of the assassinated president added:

> I believe we have overemphasized that LSD might
> be dangerous and do damage, losing sight of the fact
> that it could be very, very useful in our society when
> appropriately used.

The other senators did not agree, and the redefinition greatly reduced the probability that LSD would ever be used "appropriately." Fifteen years of use through doctors and psychologists had not produced a single case of crime or acute insanity attributable to it, but in the future there were to be many reports in the news about persons who killed or went permanently insane under its influence. The black market made it accessible to anyone, often under terribly inadequate circumstances, and although a great portion of the alarmist information was false (such as the alleged case of six boys blinded by looking at the sun), there was no dearth of bad trips. Not following minimal precautions as to setting and company, some users experienced panic. Others should simply never have used this drug in the first place because of their peculiar temperament, but the only way to select adequate persons was to put the drug under the control of competent people, while the law had decided that no one was competent.

Many defended the value of the "trip" otherwise, among them idols of the country's youth, who with rare unanimity favored psychedelics. Ten years after its prohibition, up to twenty million people may have been introduced to LSD in the United States and Europe, and the number of crimes or fatal accidents caused by its use in that decade hardly reached that produced by alcohol in one single day. In fact, what was intolerable in visionary drugs was not that they produced addiction or intoxication; it was what Octavio Paz described in *Corriente Alterna* (1967):

> The authorities do not behave toward them as if they wished to eradicate a damaging vice, but as if they wished to eradicate a dissidence. What they demonstrate is ideological zeal; they are punishing a heresy, not a crime.

And the worst heresy was a natural religion in the classic style, without any puritanism. The alarm was noticeable in a report filed in 1969 by a certain newspaperwoman regarding hippie communes in San Francisco:

> They practice cults in which blessings are done with LSD instead of the host, and where the Sex god is adored. And they dare ask the Supreme Court to recognize the constitutionality of these habits!

The link between psychedelia and antimilitarism was no less offensive, as well as the links in general with simultaneous criticisms of bourgeois and proletarian ideals. It appeared as if the Club des Haschischiens had given up its headquarters in that small Parisian hotel to open thousands of branches in developed countries, all of them conspiring without restraint against the reigning order of the times, even though at the same time that sector was creative, domestic, and pacific, producing the most profitable novelties in music, sculpture, literature, fashion, trade, and interpersonal relations.

In general, the apogee of this counterculture coincided with the affluent industrial society, where excess profits allowed millions of young people to go on pilgrimages all over the world, and many others to marginate themselves, preferring to live off the abundant leftovers rather than bite into the bait of consumerism. The year 1968 was a critical moment in the consciousness of those excess profits; it was also the year of the great student revolts in the United States and Europe. The end of the movement began with the austerity measures taken during the advent of the petroleum crisis in1973, which began incessantly to reduce those margins available to "take to the road." The societal model in place in postwar times—an ample middle class, with narrow bands of the rich and the poor above and below—began to trend toward a different model, a much harsher one, with some nouveau riche surrounded by multitudes of the new poor. The change in circumstances required other drugs as well as other vital responses.

Resting on a return to rural life and the simplicity of mores, psychedelia represented a rather naive option, compensated by a formidable success at the level of taste, since the average person—especially the young one—looked at those people with more fascination than rejection, and adopted their modes as soon as they could be divested of subversion and framed simply as something "modern." It was also true that for many, it was a cause too old, too premature, or too radical, without an organization behind it capable of enforcing effective changes. Its objective

was to empower the spontaneous, based on confidence in a freedom and an individual liberty that referred back to Rousseau's
thesis on the noble savage. When the welfare state began to exhibit
the first symptoms of crisis, cutting back on social entitlements
and auguring a time of humiliation for those not succeeding in
becoming rich, the psychedelic contingents found themselves with
the option of having to rejoin the mainstream, going from hippie
to yuppie, or else accepting existence as nostalgic fossils, living in
the memory of a world gone by.

The rebellion, however, had shaken the pharmacratic structure
that had been in place since the forties, with easy and comfortable
distinctions between decorous psychopharmaceuticals ("medicines," "food supplements") and the not-so-decorous ones ("narcotics"). The rebels had proposed an alternative pharmacopoeia
that was neither decorous or indecorous, and although thousands
of them were arrested and convicted each year for possession of
marijuana and LSD, it became impossible to continue to pretend
that the drugs sold by drugstores and supermarkets were any safer.
All quarters began to demand a new international standard, not
only for "narcotics" but for any drugs affecting mood and mind,
and this led, as we shall see, to an even more dramatic phase in
the history of Prohibition.

To take a bird's-eye view of the situation, the battle against
psychedelics was a conflict between civil rights and authoritar-
ian tradition. The end result was to be a material defeat of the
libertarians, accompanied by a moral defeat of their enemies. As
if two opponents in a duel had wounded each other at the same
time, one was falling physically injured, while the honor of the
other one, his "fair play," was put in grave doubt. Prohibitionist
arguments as such had never held credibility among scientists or
among medical or legal theoreticians, but now that credibility was
also doubted by much larger sectors of society.

The period of pharmacratic peace (1930–1960) had been
followed by an openly rebellious phase (1960–1975), and the future
offered a repetition of the phenomenon. In the rest of the world,
events were to follow a similar course one decade later.

CHAPTER SIXTEEN

Return of the Repressed

When the war against psychedelics was most intense, the Convention on Psychotropic Substances of 1971 was held in Vienna, and its special novelty was that the participating nations promised to watch over "judgment, perception, and states of mind." This implies a great change, since the nations signing The Hague Conventions of 1912 and 1914 had undertaken only to avoid the abuse of narcotic or addictive drugs.

Since the narcotic concept, as well as that of addiction, had been discarded by WHO, and the new drugs to be prohibited (LSD and its derivatives) had no addictive capacity, the new regulations that governed psychotropics (from *psyche,* "mind," and *tropia,* "modification") fell into four categories: Schedule I, substances without any medical or scientific use; Schedule II, substances with some medical uses; Schedule III, substances with substantial medical/scientific uses; and Schedule IV, substances with many scientific and medical uses. To obtain its compounds listed in Schedule I would entail overwhelming requirements from even the most competent toxicologists or therapists, while the rest could be manufactured and sold with medical prescriptions. The compounds in Schedules I and II were also subjected to international supervision and to the control of production volumes.

The substances included in Schedule I had a psychedelic profile in common. Those in the other lists were stimulants, sedatives, and narcotics. Even though they might be addictive and were incomparably more toxic than those in Schedule I, they had in their favor the fact that they were not linked to social or individual rebellion. And since at that time the most abused drugs were stimulant amines (amphetamine, dexamphetamine, methamphetamine), barbiturates, and some hypnotics, those pharmaceuticals were included in Schedules II and III. This implied that they could continue to be sold with a simple prescription, but—in contrast to the psychotropics included in Schedule IV—annual accounts of production by country would be required, following a quota system that would soon render them unavailable in drugstores. Since something similar already was occurring with synthetic and semisynthetic opiates, and with other very active stimulants, the net effect was to restrict a good part of the psycho-pharmaceuticals that had been used by law-abiding citizens since the thirties.

There was an alternative market for tranquilizers of the Valium type (which escaped inclusion in the 1971 convention for a decade and a half) and for some stimulants (with little euphoric value) not subject to restriction. But readaptation was slow, and in the interim, the field was ripe for the old infernal drugs to reappear. As a consolation, alcohol intoxication was still available, seasoned with coffee and tobacco, and the consumption of those drugs was effectively reaching historic maximums. In 1970 the Annual Statistics of the United Nations reported annual wine production as thirty billion liters, beer production as seventy billion, and liquor production as twenty billion: a yearly consumption of alcoholic beverages of some thirty-five liters per capita—including children, elders, and the abstemious—complemented by one thousand cigarettes and ten kilos of coffee.

Let us see what happened with heroin, cocaine, and hemp derivatives.

In 1972, when each year American administrations had deprived half a million citizens of their liberty for marijuana

possession, the attorney general denounced a new and unforeseen threat:

> In 1961 we had about 50,000 heroin addicts. Now we
> estimate we have 560,000.

From 1961 to 1971, federal agencies had spent $1 billion in
"repression and rehabilitation," rounded out by an additional
$6 billion contributed through Governor Rockefeller to face the
problem in New York, the location "most affected by the plague."
Nevertheless, for every needle-using addict in New York in 1961,
there were 125 in 1972. The amount could be considered inflated
by enforcement agencies, to underline their heroic overworked
conditions; in any case, in that year five FBI agents were brought
to trial and convicted of selling heroin at low prices in low-income neighborhoods in New York. Eldridge Cleaver, leader of the
radical blacks, suggested that agents blamed orders received from
their superiors, although they opted for silence.

Not only the United States but also Europe received, from
about 1964 to 1972, supplies of inexpensive and almost pure
heroin, not seen since the forties and never to be seen since. The
supplies were not much in demand, because those wishing to
remain legal used opiates from drugstores, while the psychedelic
community exhibited an Olympian disdain for any kind of
opiate.

The sudden increase noted in the United States would be
duplicated in Europe some ten years later; Spain, for example,
had 884 addicts in 1972—all of middle age, maintained with legal
supplies and without a single criminal case—while in 1983 the
Interior Ministry reported 100,000 addicts, and three-fourths of
all crimes against property were attributed to them.

The official explanation given for the availability of this supply of heroin in the United States and later in Europe, generous
and not interfered with, was that enforcement agencies were
fighting the use of LSD and later marijuana, and thus were unable to handle two things at once. The real fact is that the ritual

consumption of heroin—the junkie mystique—went along with a high degree of police control, thanks to informants paid with drugs and immune to prosecution. Sales of an ounce of marijuana a day would support the cultivator, and barely the distributor; while sales of an ounce of heroin would support twenty persons for a week, all of them subject to blackmail. Even further, the junkie fully accepted being considered a mixture of wretch and poor victim, fulfilling the prophecies of Prohibition with the first, and providing a market for therapy with the second; the marijuana user did not declare himself to be either a devil or a sick man. Finally, addiction could be exported to ghettos, converting potential political explosiveness in those neighborhoods into a problem of citizens' "lack of safety."

Whatever the reasons for such an excess of heroin, it reached America through the Mediterranean and Asiatic connections, and the latter—principal supplier of the American market—continued to depend on the CIA. As a high official in that agency made clear, the deterioration of the Vietnam situation demanded that an underground war be maintained by means of pro-Western groups, which were sometimes forced to survive by means of anomalous operations. Among these was the export of some five hundred tons of opium from the Golden Triangle: a tribute demanded by Generals Li We-huan and Chang Chi-fu, leaders of two guerrilla groups, from native populations in the area in order to procure arms and munitions to protect them from China. Refined in Thailand, a part of the heroin was shipped to the United States, while the rest remained for use by troops in Vietnam. In 1972, 20 percent of the American expeditionary forces consumed this pharmaceutical, and the high command was so aware of it that it organized "quarantines" of those units in Europe and Australia before allowing them to return home. One year earlier, the press had revealed that one method of exporting the drug was to stuff the corpses of dead repatriated soldiers with it, several of these having been discovered at Norton Air Force Base in California, with an average amount of twenty-five kilos in each.

In a tense climate, which began to put Nixon's competence

in doubt, Congress decided to create a consulting group, the National Commission on Marijuana and Drug Abuse, to report on the true state of affairs. A national survey was run, based on anonymous replies to one question ("Which drugs have you taken during the past week?"), and the results indicated that some two million Americans had taken heroin during the previous week. That number exceeded the most alarmist police estimates by a factor of four, suggesting that occasional use of the drug also existed. A new global survey, run by the National Institute for Drug Abuse (NIDA), substituted "the prior week" by "at any time," and the answers indicated that 5 percent of adults and 1 percent of adolescents—about eight million—had consumed heroin.

This put in question the supposition that nobody, or hardly anybody, could exercise self-control with such a euphoria-producing drug. There was something else, because in that same year, with eight million Americans introduced to heroin, only 14,476 submitted themselves to voluntary detoxification. Even though many more persons were classified as addicts in psychiatric hospitals and prisons, their cooperation lasted only as long as their detention. Those who asked to be cured—0.18 percent of the number that consumed or had consumed heroin, or 0.00018 percent of the total population—supported a multi-billion dollar repression and rehabilitation apparatus. Half a dozen institutions in the country, principally medical and judicial ones, concluded from these surveys that neither the enforcement nor the rehabilitation agencies came even remotely close to minimal expectations of efficiency.

Nixon and his special assistant, R. Jaffe, responded with a "war on drugs on all fronts," particularly in two initiatives. The first was to give the green light to Turkish generals to dismantle their democracy in return for $30 million a year and a promise to remove all legal cultivation of poppies in their country (even though these were producing $300 million in hard currency and employing tens of thousands of peasant families). The second was to present methadone as "national ammunition" and a "counterrevolutionary drug," putting in place a policy of giving it away free to anyone who declared himself or herself as incapable of living without heroin. Nixon promoted maintenance programs with methadone because, in his own words:

> Remaining addicted to heroin represents a concession to weakness and defeat in the crusade against drugs, which no doubt would lead to erosion of our most cherished values of human dignity.

Some such as Dr. T. Szasz, would immediately reply that this was tantamount to maintaining that an alcoholic would be cured of whiskey addiction by giving him gin. The example was exact even to the last detail, because as whiskey is easier for the body to take than gin, heroin produces fewer side effects than methadone. Furthermore, the street addict usually took a very adulterated form of heroin ("brown sugar"), and substituting methadone for it multiplied a real dependency. When substitution was put in place in 1973, therefore, deaths by overdose of methadone exceeded those of heroin. This mortality rate was later reduced by certain precautions, such as requiring subjects to consume their doses while at the dispensary itself, but even then the equilibrium was unclear, because the majority of heroin addicts died of adulteration, and overdoses of methadone correspond actually to that drug, alone or mixed with others.

In 1977 some hundred thousand federally supported Americans were methadone addicts. To answer protests that the methadone chemical prison was harsher than that of heroin (although much less euphoric, which led to guzzling up other drugs), the government explained that it granted what was asked of it—a potent and legal narcotic—while offering heroin would imply a genocide. In fact, the administration had for three years been allowing the use of synthetic opiates, and the NIDA survey mentioned shows that in 1978 there were twenty-five million occasional users and two million frequent users.

Counter to official assumptions, surveys had shown that the correlation between heroin consumption and addiction was not statistically significant. Three other assumptions were left: that those labeled as heroin addicts in fact consumed that drug, that they were young and unwillingly drawn in by those who corrupted them, and that they frequently died of overdosing. But from 1973, when street samples of the drug began to be tested, until 1990, only 5 percent proved pure, and the remaining 95 percent proved to be many other things (lactose, strychnine, cacao, quinine, opiates, drugstore tranquilizers, sodium borate, rat poison, etc.). These fraudulent substances were sold at $100 per gram, and it is curious that many junkies emigrated from countries where pure and inexpensive heroin prescriptions could still be obtained—such as England until 1974—because such circumstances did not allow them a stage for their drama.

The second assumption—that heroin addicts were principally adolescents, involuntary victims of those who inducted them—did not apply either. Research suggested that those tending to junkie status were an almost fixed percentage of society, as invariable as the percentage of those going to psychiatrists or practicing magic, and that this type of person not only anticipated induction but took great pains during many months of trying to reach even a slight level of dependence. Furthermore, toward 1977, most addicts were between thirty and forty years of age, or else belonged to the low-income strata, or they were spoiled children who had drifted into psychedelics because it was fashionable to do so, had experienced bad "trips," and had finally found a sense of identity in irresponsibility.

The third supposition—that heroin addicts always died, frequently of heroin overdoses—erred because of the high percentage of adulteration. If someone died after ingesting all at once a full bottle of watered whiskey with a 5 percent whiskey content, no one would attribute the death to an excess of alcohol, but to some other factor, probably linked to the water; why then attribute the deaths of heroin addicts to heroin, instead of the adulterating compounds? One could suppose that here and there a pure batch might be present, but in the United States, for example, from 1973 to 1986 the average purity of street heroin was

6.3 percent (in 1980), and the least pure 3.8 percent (in 1976). Even though the overdose rate was highest in Washington, D.C. in 1981, 1.7 percent of junkies being killed then, autopsies demonstrated that those deaths were due to adulteration of the product with quinine.

Last, it is significant that the policies of the police in heroin matters had been unanimous since the seventies in considering that adulteration and scarcity of the product protected the user and that the opposite put him at risk. B. Besinger, the first DEA director, so stated at his swearing-in ceremony:

> There are two fundamental tools in the fight against drugs: reduce their purity, and raise their price.

Paradoxically, the strategy of enforcers coincided item by item with that of the illegal dealers. An adulterated and expensive heroin market would end by multiplying by a factor of one hundred the number of deaths attributed to overdoses.

When the psychedelic rebellion was still fashionable, although LSD and its derivatives began to seem excessive for the new era, cocaine reappeared as the "adult" and even "civilized" drug. In the seventies, the United States was very sensitive to any alternative pharmacological offer, and for a while imports of this drug from several points in Latin America became the business of a few private, non-Mafia persons, who made one or two trips abroad each year, buying small amounts, and subsisting with some profit. Consumers of it in 1970 were some five million American occasional users who secured reasonably pure cocaine at affordable prices, with few cases of intoxication. In 1970, for example, 80 deaths were attributed to heroin, 137 to barbiturates, 553 to alcohol, 10 to amphetamine, and none to cocaine.

Five years later, with Gerald Ford as president, the White Book on drugs prepared by the administration considered cocaine "a minor problem" comparable only to marijuana, defining it as a much less dangerous substance than other illegal drugs, and of course less dangerous than alcohol, barbiturates, and amphetamines. This period of bonanza for small-time smugglers and consumers, however, was soon to come to an end, because contraband and distributor clans appeared and did not hesitate to use aggression, adulteration of the product without scruples, and bribery to avoid interference. The first arrested dealers of any importance turned out to be high-ranking officials of the Batista government in exile, and soon thereafter, some links began to be detected between those "anti-Castro" elements and the CIA, since some of the former avoided trial when the Justice Department was informed that they were "important to the national interest." Ten years later, those links operated in the case of the Nicaraguan Contras, financed by Colombian cartels in order to allow the passage into the United States of small planes loaded with cocaine, although in this case it was not the CIA that was present but rather Lieutenant Colonel O. North, and the National Security Council after him, consisting of the President, the Vice-President, the Secretary of Defense, and the Chiefs of Staff of the three branches of the armed forces.

Two years were sufficient for the five million occasional users to become more than thirty million, and another two for the number to reach 42 percent of adults. Just as heroin socialized the problem, cocaine socialized well-being at the most obvious level, in the mirror looked into by those who sniffed it with a $100 bill or a small gold tube, feeling part of a select atmosphere of pleasure and worldliness. It was also a way to imitate the marginalized without becoming marginalized oneself, with a substance that did not entail a "trip" and that formed part of the halo of the successful, used by artists, executives, and politicians to maintain their status.

The most evident solution was to eradicate the coca bush where it grew. The plantations in Bolivia, Peru, and Ecuador, however—the traditional producers—were now joined by others in Guatemala, Venezuela, Paraguay, Chile, and some areas of the Brazilian Amazon. Panama, Nicaragua, Costa Rica, Colombia, Mexico, Brazil, Cuba, Haiti, the Dominican Republic, and other small countries in the Caribbean stored, transported, refined, or laundered the money from the traffic, and the DEA began to openly accuse the CIA of placing obstacles in the fight against the enormous traffic, since a sizable portion of it was in the hands of "antisubversive" groups. All Latin American nations outwardly pretended to fight actively against cocaine, but the margins derived from it formed not only a substantial part of their economy but also a way of positioning the policeman from the North in a position similar to that of China when it prohibited opium imports, compensating a recent history of military invasions, political blackmail, and merciless economic exploitation. Since the first Roosevelt, with his policy of "the big stick," Anglo-Saxon America had systematically promoted corruption south of the Rio Grande, and now it was reaping the harvest of that seed. Its crusade against certain drugs offered the weak an unforeseen opportunity to trade "an eye for an eye," and they were not to miss that opportunity.

On the other hand, those receiving the profit were not Indian peasants or even the different national economies, because a policy of selective repression soon liquidated the small dealers and cottage industries, consolidating monopoly prices for the higher echelons of the army and the police, the true owners of the trade, who occasionally exposed laboratories and contraband to cover themselves with a facade of respectability.

The other drug that took root in the United States, and a few years later in Europe, was hemp, as marijuana or as hashish. In 1972 the report of the National Commission on Marijuana and Drug Abuse advised the legalization of its consumption, based on the harmlessness of the product and the fact that it was being used by twenty-five million Americans. In 1977 a new national survey indicated that 60 percent of young adults had used marijuana or hashish at some point (68 percent, for example, had smoked tobacco at some time), and the permissiveness of the older adults increased in the same proportion. In 1979 the National Survey on Drug Abuse showed that 68 percent of young adults were familiar with hemp derivatives and that half of them used them frequently.

At the same time, those thirty-five or forty million consumers, regular or sporadic, did not produce proven delinquent incidents, and fatal intoxications were absent. Between May 1976 and April 1977, official data mention 10 deaths from hashish oil (a super-concentrated form of hemp, toxic because of the compounds used in its extraction), while 310 were attributed to methadone, 2,530 to alcohol, 2,700 to barbiturates, 390 to aspirin, and 880 to Valium. This last drug had been, incidentally, the principal cause of admissions into intensive care units: 54,400 cases. Except LSD-type compounds, which had never produced fatal intoxication, only cocaine then had fewer deaths than those from hemp derivatives.

Unable to supply itself sufficiently from the great plantations in Jamaica, Panama, Colombia, and Brazil, the giant market imported marijuana from Thailand as well as hashish from Afghanistan, Nepal, India, Pakistan, Turkey, Lebanon, and Morocco. But there was still a strong demand, which launched domestic cultivation of the plant, first in the West Coast states and Hawaii. Toward 1976, when J. Carter began his bid for the presidency, the United States was becoming one of the larger world producers, with the most sought-after varieties (the California "sin semilla" and the "maui"). This explains why the White House itself—in the time of G. Ford, after the resignation of Nixon—favored a change of attitude for the first time in history. Press notices appeared in which Rosalynn Carter and Betty Ford competed in cautious liberalism. According to the *New York Times* of April 3, 1976:

> The wife of the Democratic Presidential candidate said that her three older sons smoke marijuana. . . . Mrs. Carter's statements, similar to those made by Mrs. Ford, are coherent with her prior position that marijuana should be decriminalized, not necessarily legalized.

Beginning in 1976, the possession of hemp for one's own

use ceased to be illegal in California. Although not officially recognized, cultivation of the plant became a regular agricultural
endeavor within that state and in the nation as a whole. An in-
dication of the change of attitude was the fact, for example, that
the NORML association—founded with the aim of securing "absolute normalization" for the consumption of marijuana—sued
the DEA, accusing it of bribing the Mexican government with
$40 million to spray hemp plantations with Paraquat, a product
very toxic to the lungs. Instead of tossing aside the whole matter
as absurd, the White House started an investigation, the result
of which was the admission that in fact, the DEA had handed
over tons of the product to Mexico, even though no proof could
be shown that it was a poison to the respiratory tract weeks or
months after use.

This change of attitude toward hemp was not endorsed by the
DEA or by its defenders among the citizenry, who, lacking biological data on toxicity or dependence, mentioned alleged incidents
of furious lust or criminal bent among users. The most famous
case in this sense occurred during the courtmartial of Lieutenant
W. Calley for a massacre in the Vietnamese village of My Lai. The
defense stated that "the officer spent some time in a room where
others, hours before, had smoked marijuana." The slaughter of
almost one hundred defenseless persons—all of them older men,
women, and children—would not have happened, according to
the accused, without the insidious presence of that drug in the
environment.

In spite of that, from the end of the seventies until the
middle of the eighties, the perception of hemp as a "soft" drug
was unstoppable, and consumption became legal—officially or
practically—in Canada, Spain, Holland, Denmark, and parts of
the United States. It is interesting that during that same time, many
previously inveterate users became progressively less interested.
In Spain, for example, after the penal reform that distinguished
between hard and soft drugs, the possession of hashish, as well as
smoking it—even in public—stopped being dangerous, and in
doing so lost its passionate, heroic, or heretic content. Deprived

of ceremonial value, hashish stocks gathered dust in writing desks and night tables. The most notable case took place in Holland, where hemp derivatives ended up being sold freely in fifteen hundred coffee shops throughout the country, attracting marijuana users from all over Europe who were discomfited by adulteration of the products in their countries of origin. Consumption of the product by the Dutch did not, in any case, increase, and only 5 percent of the population smoked it regularly.

CHAPTER SEVENTEEN

The Era of Substitutes

After several indecisive years, the war on drugs was revived with great virulence during the eighties, an era marked by the Reagan-Thatcher duo, which began to get used to cyclical crises even though it administered a prosperity without precedent. The new thing about this prosperity was that it became ever more selective: now competition increased to the maximum, thanks to unemployment created by the automation of manufacturing processes. The welfare state seemed daily to be more and more an insufferable waste, and cutting back the so-called social expenses without reducing others consolidated areas of poverty around each prosperous center. Meanwhile, governments and the media presented illicit drugs as an apocalyptic plague and the main cause of lack of safety, and legislative bodies imposed harsher terms against their use or traffic.

So much alarm and punishment also functioned as indirect promotion, since why would the consumer pay such high prices and risk such dangers if it were not for a supreme pleasure—or at least superior to most others—to be secured as a reward? This ambiguity permeated communities rich and poor, young and old, provoking not only hypocrisy but a generalized passive resistance as well. This resistance was reflected in the speech of the oppressors themselves when they announced a war of attrition: the narco-enemy was too powerful to be defeated in the short or medium term, and what was foreseen was a long-term conflict, where not yielding ground was already a victory.

At the same time, the huge size of the commerce of manufacturing and distributing illicit drugs now generated important changes: side by side with traditional manufacturers, others appeared to embark on a search for psychotropic substances in areas where they could be found in unlimited amounts, manipulating atoms, molecules, and compounds commonly used in industry. Their discoveries would turn out to be the designer drugs—anesthetic, stimulant, and visionary—having in common their birth from Prohibition. All previous drugs had been legal at first, and later on had become illegal. This group, instead, flourished from the very beginning as an alternative offer to original ones excluded from legal commerce, and the demand for them largely depended on those originals continuing to be expensive and forbidden.

Sometimes those substances were discovered by chemists and tested in laboratories before reaching the black market; others were the fruit of domestic "kitchens," which as easily produced the targeted drug as a compound unknown until that time. As a whole, they represented the response of the black market and the rebel imagination to the exacerbation of the crusade, a response that in one decade would invent several substitutes more potent, less expensive, and almost always more toxic than each of the prior illicit drugs.

The eighties thus could be defined as the moment when drug addiction became addiction to substitutes at a worldwide level. On one hand, the monopolization of the clandestine traffic (ever more linked to secret services, armies, and the police) imposed standards of lower purity on classic drugs. On the other, the old-style traffic, based on plantations and the transport of product through borders, was complemented by clandestine chemists or just "cooks" operating within each country, offering substitutes for heroin, cocaine, LSD, and hemp.

Among designer drugs corresponding to the opiates group, china-white stands out: a generic name covering many variants of fentanyl, a synthetic opiate now used as a morphine substitute in four-fifths of surgical operations in Western clinics. Several times more active than heroin, fentanyl enjoys a relatively low toxicity in addition to formidable anesthetic powers.

Nevertheless, what began to appear as china-white was not fentanyl but a derivative of it—such as alphamethyl fentanyl or parafluor fentanyl—with an almost unreal potency, because among its many analogs there were some with up to two thousand times the activity of heroin. One cup of some of these variants was equivalent to a trunk full of morphine, and a millionth of gram would sell at fifty cents, considering that sixty or seventy micrograms were enough to achieve the same effects as an average dose of heroin. Furthermore, the synthesis of these super-anesthetics is relatively simple, starting from basic products used in the manufacture of plastics: alphamethyl styrene, formaldehyde, methylamine.

Naturally, the dissemination of china-white increased the rate of acute intoxication and death. A portion of those casualties could be attributed to the high activity of the chemical principles, though most of them were due to the filler used to provide volume or else to the random production of a neurotoxin during synthesis. This is not subject to question, since a group of people survived, who (taking pure parafluor fentanyl, for example) administered to themselves amounts up to fifty times those found in the victims of alleged overdoses.

In addition to the derivatives of fentanyl, there were various other synthetic and semisynthetic substances and indefinite numbers of analogs, with greater power than heroin, which any competent chemist could extract from legal pharmaceuticals and drugstore items. The better-known ones, because of their high euphoria-producing properties, were dihydromorphinone (Dilaudid) and 14,hydroxydihydromorphinone (Numorphan), although it seems inevitable that more would be discovered each year, as well as newer synthetic procedures to manufacture them.

Among the stimulant designer drugs were artificial cocaines with various names: coco snow, crystal caine, synth coke. In many cases these were variants of katine and katinone, alkaloids of khat—a plant consumed by millions in Somalia, Yemen, and the eastern coast of Africa. In the Far East, ice became very popular, a simple methamphetamine used in liquid form as a drop at the end of a cigarette. Its activity assured an effect lasting several hours with a single administration, or lasting a whole day or more with higher doses, causing overexcitement moderated by the ingestion of large quantities of alcohol and drugstore sedatives. It was used principally by the Japanese, Chinese, and Indonesians.

Although ice addicts were more numerous, no other stimulant designer drug became more famous than crack, usually a basic paste of cocaine amalgamated with sodium bicarbonate. This name was applied to the basic paste as well, which is cocaine before "washing" or purification with ether and acetone. To transmute cocaine again into basic paste is a very simple operation: only ammonia needs to be added. When it is smoked in pipes, or when it is heated on foil and the smoke from it is inhaled, crack produces a euphoria superior to that of cocaine, although shorter. The typical user has characteristics similar to those of an opiate junkie, tending to dramatize a situation of irresistible dependence, he is incapable of self-control and, like the alcoholic, continues to take the drug until there is no more or until fatigue overcomes him, sometimes causing sleeplessness for days.

The toxicity of crack appears to be very high, judging by the number of deaths attributed to it. For example, in 1989, with forty times fewer users than cocaine, it produced fifteen deaths for each one attributed to cocaine, suggesting that fatal poisoning is some six hundred times more probable. In fact, the toxicity of these chemicals is not much different. Similarly to the china-white situation, crack has been consumed by several control groups without acute incidents, and the high percentage of compulsive use derives rather from the fact that crack is the stimulant of the poor, used by the less favored sectors of the population. If cocaine represents the luxury of the successful, basic paste nd crack are the luxuries of the miserable, befitting a substitute more active and ten or twelve times less expensive than the original.

In effect, three to five kilos of basic paste are needed to produce one kilo of cocaine, and the process does not require either very expensive or hard-to-work-with solvents. If we also consider the generous filler of sodium bicarbonate, an almost cost-free product, one can understand that by 1985 a vial with crack crystals cost between three and five dollars, while a gram of cocaine cost between one and two hundred dollars. That is why in addition to the powerful Mafia of this drug, a second one was to rise, capable of reaching into poor pockets as efficiently as the former milked the rich ones.

The most peculiar item in the appearance and diffusion of crack is that it derives from restrictions imposed on the availability of ether and acetone—substances necessary to transform basic paste into cocaine hydrochlorate—following instructions from the American DEA, later adopted by the UN. Before international authorities decided to restrict the use of these precursors, in the cocaine-producing countries it was as expensive to obtain and store ether and acetone stocks as cocaine. Further reduction of the availability of those precursors was sufficient to cause them to start exporting basic paste, and the tricky contortions of the American black market did the rest. Crack is a result of the war on cocaine, specifically of the measures taken against the solvents required for its purification.

It is also interesting to note that the panic provoked by the "unforeseen epidemic" and the harshening of sentences caused not only a lowering of the average age of users, with high rates of juvenile addicts, but also a rapid increase in young dealers. In Washington, Detroit, New York, Los Angeles, and other great American cities, the penal measures proposed by Reagan and Bush were to multiply from four to eight times the number of camels under the age of sixteen. The same thing had happened in the case of heroin, when in the middle of the fifties, the Narcotics Control Act imposed draconian penalties on consumers.

Even then, official documentation omits important and

relevant details, such as the fact that juvenile sellers often become so in order to help families besieged by poverty, that they are often the most intelligent (considering their school records prior to their becoming professionals), and that many of them do not consume what they sell. This documentation does not mention, either, that unemployment among black and Chicano young men increased during the Reagan-Bush era to almost 50 percent; that minimum wages, adjusted for inflation, reached their lowest level since 1955; that the number of unskilled, low-paid workers increased from three million to seventeen million between 1979 and 1989; that student grants and loans were reduced by 20 percent, while education costs practically doubled; and that, in general, the budget for training and employment programs—essential for disadvantaged youth—was frozen or eliminated.

Among the psychedelic drugs discovered or distributed in the eighties, there was a wide variety of substances, often characterized by a benzene ring of the mescaline type in their structure. Usually identified by an acronym such as DOM, DOET, DOB, TMA, MDE, MBDB, DMT, or MDA, the one with the most notoriety in this decade was MDMA, or Ecstasy, a drug difficult to place in the visionary group because it opens up the doors of empathy more than it does those of vision.

Used since the middle of the seventies by Anglo-Saxon psychologists and psychiatrists, MDMA reached the summit of its legal prestige in 1984, when it became the emblem of the New Age movement and its popular version, the rave, a more contested form—with overtones of hippiedom—concentrated in discotheques and suburban locations, with a Spanish version known as the "cod route." Until that time, no bad trips or serious intoxications were reported, even though thousands used it, but in 1985 its fame led the DEA to declare it out of bounds, not only for the general public but for the medical establishment as well. This initiative provoked criticism from various therapists, based upon MDMA's "almost incredible capacity to facilitate subjective communication and access to repressed material." The DEA responded that forbidding its use "did not depend on its physical or psychical damaging effects, but rather on the numbers of people who might want to use MDMA."

In a climate of international expectation, the matter was taken to the Expert Committee at WHO, which made a statement beginning:

> There is no available data about propensity for clinical abuse, or about social or public health or epidemiological problems related to this substance. There is no well-defined therapeutic use, but many professionals affirm it has great value as a psychotherapeutic agent.

The Committee went as far as to define MDMA as a substance that was "intriguing and deserving of further research"—terms never before applied to a psychoactive drug—but confirmed the criteria of the DEA by including it in Schedule I, the repository of drugs without medical use, which cannot even be self-tested by toxicologists or psychotherapists. In the following year, 1986, extensive amounts of MDMA were available in the black market, almost always adulterated with more toxic products, which began to lead to deaths. Since then, it has been sold in bars and discotheques as an aphrodisiac (which it never was or ever would be), at prices comparable to those of heroin or cocaine, and by 1990 it was—along with hemp derivatives—the illegal euphoric agent preferred by middle-class youth in the United States and Europe. For example, in 1993 almost five million capsules were confiscated in Spain, most of them being actually MDA or another analogue, usually more toxic organically, and usually adulterated.

Ecstasy's fame as an aphrodisiac generally derives not from the more or less informed user but usually from its detractors, who seem to ignore the vigorous marketing promotion that results from that labeling. Nevertheless, designer psychedelics may have come closer to a libido-enhancing substance with other drugs, specifically 2CB, or nexus (also known as afro), which in some ways combines the effects of LSD and MDMA and enhances orgasms. Nexus promised to imitate and even exceed the success of Ecstasy, because although it was forbidden in the United States, but not yet in many parts of the world, some amounts began to appear on the black market. Inexpensive and easy to produce, 2C-B (bromodimethoxy phenethylamine) had been tested for two decades by small experimental groups without producing incidents of acute intoxication or lasting psychoses, but it is a drug requiring careful usage, which induces terror when overdosed and, under restrictions, could generate many bad trips.

The same could be said about some thousand other drugs with a psychedelic profile, from the ultrapotent STP—with effects lasting one or two days—to DMT, which gives rise to very intense visionary trances during five or ten minutes. Among these designer pharmaceuticals, other much older ones have reappeared, such as peyote, yagé, and iboga—frequent vehicles of sacramental communion for religious cults in North and South America, and in Africa. The sacramental use of peyote, protected in a zigzag history by the American Constitution, is on the rise among Native Americans in the prairies, and the bwiti cult concentrated around Gabon, Guinea, and Cameroon, seems to be increasing as well. None of those religions, however, enjoys as many devotees as the Santo Daime church, originally from Brazil and now with branches over most of the world. Its sacrament is yagé or ayahuasca, containing DMT as well as other ingredients.

The decade of the eighties without a doubt covers the greatest institutional effort ever made to repress the use of illegal drugs. The crusade was already a phenomenon of global scale, and its result was an alarm without precedent. The American federal government alone—independently of state funds—spent millions on repression. Following the Reagan-Bush initiatives, it was not unheard of for children to report their parents or brothers for cultivating marijuana or possessing cocaine, or for parents to kill or wound their own children when they found them using an illicit drug.

What the administration asked for, as a *Time* editorial mentioned in 1986, was a "civil war within the home." The so-called Enemy Within substituted for the old communist enemy, and the initiative to liquidate it at any cost—even by suspending civil liberties guaranteed by the Constitution—took on titanic proportions, since the most conservative estimates of users placed them at 25 percent of the population. Surrealist aspects permeated the scene; for example, in the trial of D. Steinberg, accused of importing tons of marijuana from Thailand, the prime witness was a professional criminal (who confessed to fifteen murders), given immunity in exchange for his testimony. The prosecuting attorney was first suspended for using barbiturates and for drunk driving and later dismissed for cocaine use, while the policeman who captured Steinberg was fired before the hearing of the case was over for trying to induce a colleague to become a dealer. Meanwhile the terminated officer had "lost" one kilo of confiscated cocaine two years before, and shortly thereafter "lost" a further kilo and a half. In the same year, 1985, Dr. C. K. Drew, a captain in the health services department, was dismissed from the army when random tests revealed that she had self-administered a certain analgesic commonly available in drugstores. After she proved that her dentist had given her a prescription for it months before, Dr. Drew alleged that she had taken only three pills of the prescribed four, and that she had decided to use the fourth on that day to face a painful menstrual period. But the military court ruled that self-medication—even only once and with a legal drug—was improper for a physician.

In a climate of excited alarm, the global reflection of similar cases inevitably yielded paradoxical results. With the whole country in a war against cocaine—now the "number one enemy of America"—the circulating amount of that drug in the United States reached such proportions that in 1984 its price had gone down by 66 percent. In January of 1988, with the army functioning as supplementary customs agent and innumerable police involved in the pursuit, prices tumbled another two-thirds, with a kilo pegged at some $40,000, whereas a decade earlier, in the "permissive"

Carter era, the cost was five times higher. Hundreds of tons were distributed without a single large internal dealer being identified or convicted. On one hand, billions of dollars were designated for enforcement and repressive activities while on the other, the nation was simply saturated with cocaine, to the point where Colombian, Peruvian, and Bolivian exporters decided to attempt to open European markets. In Spain, for example, the amounts confiscated in 1988 were four times greater than those confiscated in the previous two decades.

The same can be said about marijuana, demonized again by official circles upon the accession of Ronald Reagan to the presidency. In 1982 the Supreme Court confirmed a forty-year prison sentence for possession of marijuana valued at $200, previously declared "cruel and unusual punishment" by two courts of appeal. The cultivation of marijuana quickly increased nevertheless, and—according to the DEA itself—exceeded the value of the whole grain harvest, feeding a large underground economy. Hydroponics cultivation, done indoors with totally automated equipment, allowed up to five yearly harvests of varieties ever richer in THC, the active principle, and savvy producers could obtain hundreds of kilos by simply equipping a large room or garage for that purpose.

A similar thing happened with heroin, initially displaced by cocaine at the decade's beginning but regaining momentum after 1988. In any case, no other fact was more meaningful and loaded with repercussions as the flowering of designer drugs, which placed the pharmacological crusade as a war against general chemistry itself, a difficult enterprise to drive forward without setback. The first of these has been the flooding of the world with analogues and substitutes, carrying greater profit margins for the manufacturers and distributors and higher risks of intoxication for the user. Designer drugs—literally born from Prohibition—and a new golden age for organized crime, are largely responsible for the increase in overdosing and poisoning due to adulterants that is noticeable everywhere, especially where the crusade is most active. In Spain, for example, from 1980 to

1990, some seven thousand people, excluding suicides, died of involuntary intoxication with heroin. Most deaths were due to product impurities, although sometimes they were due to batches of high purity, and most of the victims young. From 1920 to 1930, when opium and morphine were sold in drugstores and even in herb shops, there was not a single case of fatal involuntary intoxication with these drugs.

CHAPTER EIGHTEEN

Some Aspects of the Problem

W henever important distribution routes are identified, in most cases links with political entities and secret services also surface. As we have seen, this was obvious in the cases of one of the largest providers of LSD, and in that one of the two "connections" for the manufacture and distribution of heroin. It was no less applicable in the case of cocaine; Senator C. Kerry, chairman of the House subcommittee on terrorism and drugs, considered it "proven" in the famous "Irangate," one of the ramifications of which was the financing of the Nicaraguan Contras in exchange for permission to import that drug into the United States by means of aircraft loaded by the Medellin cartel.

Still surrounded by fog, which only now has begun to dispel, the rare large dealer identified before falling from grace has an interesting profile. From information provided by the DEA itself, the cocaine chieftain Alberto Sicilia-Falcon was originally an anti-Castro militant with a passport renewed in Cuba, who deposited money in Swiss and Russian banks, had CIA contacts, and moved with perfect impunity in Mexico with an identity card as special agent issued by a department of the Mexican government. Also according to the DEA, Lung Shing, top man in heroin, was the son of the last feudal lord of Yunan, the Chinese province traditionally dedicated to poppy cultivation, and he enjoyed good relationships with the CIA and other intelligence services, not to mention a clear preeminence over military groups controlling the Golden Triangle.

Beyond "deluxe" intermediaries, such as Sicilia-Falcon and Lung Shing, what lay at the core of the matter, before the illicit drug traffic reached its present proportions, was an exchange of prohibited substances for military arms and influence. Since the beginning of the seventies, however, what these people have been involved in is a business, the net profits of which exceed those of nuclear and fossil fuels combined. Protected by anonymity, there is no lack of hints that this business continues to be concentrated in fewer and fewer hands, by means of international councils that gradually merge to handle the needs of production, distribution, and laundering of the resultant cash. We do not know for sure to what degree this underground empire has already become a single syndicate, such as that in existence in the last few years of alcohol prohibition, or whether it is still in the process of formation, with independent and perhaps even conflicting branches. But its nature would incline to the first option, following a trend to monopoly actively encouraged by illegality. Let's consider two cases.

Nugan Hand Inc., a holding company that was one of the largest in the Pacific Rim in terms of sales volume, went bankrupt in 1980, ruining several thousand small investors in the process. Since the banker F. Nugan died apparently as a suicide, shot with a hunting gun, and his partner, M. Hand, disappeared without a trace, along with a significant part of the company archives, the Australian government named two investigative commissions, which reported involvement of the holding company in the following activities:

1. Affairs with persons known or suspected to have connections with drugs, to whom the company had contributed funds in several countries.
2. Intensive banking operations in Florida ... including a number of accounts confiscated by narcotic agents.

3. Active involvement in negotiations related to the supply of military equipment to several countries and persons.
4. Along with indications that point to a connection to the FBI (which had systematically placed obstacles to the investigation, alleging "reasons of national security") there was circumstantial and direct evidence of connections with the CIA and other American entities related to intelligence services.

Among the dealers connected to Nugan Hand Inc. were A. Saffron and T. Clark, "key members of organized crime in Asia and Australia," according to police, as well as J. Fratianno and F. Tieri, well-known members of the American Cosa Nostra. The initial mentors of the Nugan Hand Bank had been the Australian P. Abeles and the American D. K. Ludwig, at that time world transportation moguls. Nonetheless, the top executives of the company were strikingly odd. The president of Nugan Hand Inc. in Hawaii was General E. F. Black, counterespionage veteran and former member of the National Security Council. The president in Manila was General L. J. Manor, specialist in "countersubversion and special operations," supreme chief of Pacific operations in 1976. The president of Nugan Hand in Washington was General E. Cocke Jr., former president of the International Bank for Reconstruction and Development. The director of Nugan Hand in Taiwan was D. Holmgren, manager as well of an airline company established by the CIA to supply guerrillas in the Golden Triangle. The director of Nugan Hand in Saigon was R. Jantzen, director of the CIA in Vietnam until the American evacuation. The top president of the holding company was Admiral E. P. Yates, chief of strategic planning at the Pentagon for Asia and the Pacific.

But that wasn't all. Nugan Hand Inc. had one counsel and two associate counsels. One was W. MacDonald, former financial director of the CIA; the other was G. Pauker, Kissinger's personal assistant (under Nixon), and later Brzezinski's (under

Carter). Their chief counsel was W. Colby, former director general of the CIA (immediately before Bush); it was Colby who installed Hand as Nugan's partner. Hand was a person without a university education who had worked as a military instructor in the Golden Triangle. Police found a piece of paper with Colby's and Wilson's telephone numbers on it next to Nugan's corpse; House Representative Robert Wilson had just retired, after having served as chairman of the House Armed Services Committee.

Of course, the top executive echelon of the company was not aware of its true activities or of the black hole it ended up being for most of its small shareholders. In 1986 the files of this case were turned into a book by one of the editors of the *Wall Street Journal,* and before publication, presented to the surviving executives of Nugan Hand Inc. for their review. None of them chose to comment, except Admiral Yates, president of the holding company, and his words are instructive:

> There has been no proof that any of us were involved in, or knew about, any traffic in drugs, illegal sales of arms, or money laundering. . . . We are the true patriots, and our only imprudence was to have trusted in a colleague. To stir up this matter further, voluntarily or involuntarily, would benefit the interests of the Soviet Union and the disinformation services of the KGB.

A memorandum written and signed by Yates shows that he personally led the negotiations to have the Sultan of Brunei—considered the richest man on the planet—invest in Nugan Hand, offering him "a system foreign to any political change in your country, with maximum security for special operations."

By the time the Nugan Hand maze exploded, another global one was ready to do so. The International Bank of Commerce and Credit (IBCC) was called upon to become the first financial power in Islam, with shareholders such as the sheik of Dubai, the Saudi royal family, and the Gokal brothers, transportation magnates. The Pakistani founder, Agha Hassan Abedi, had a good pretext for increasing his geopolitical power with the Soviet invasion of Afghanistan. In 1985 the IBBC had more than four hundred branches in over seventy countries and was the seventh largest bank in the world. Its influence in the United States was so large that it ended up secretly in control of First American Bankshares, with three hundred branches from New York to Florida, presided over by C. Clifford, former Defense Secretary and personal counsel to various presidents.

Some bank executives were imprisoned in 1988 in the United States for laundering drug money, although the company continued to function without interference. In the spring of 1990, a Price-Waterhouse audit, while J. Major was Chancellor of the Exchequer, determined that the company, at least in England, was "in complete chaos." But the government did not intervene, an abstention that would later be used to criticize it as collaborating in the embezzlement of some $10 billion away from the small and medium customers of English banks. Not until the summer of 1991 did the governor of the Bank of England call the IBCC "a rotten fraud" and—in an unprecedented operation in banking history—all of the bank's offices were immediately closed in Europe and the United States. It was the greatest fraud of all time, and with the scandal, revelations arrived that the company had a "black net" formed by more than fifteen hundred employees, dedicated to buying and selling arms and currencies, espionage, kidnapping, and murder as a coverup for traffic in drugs and the laundering of money.

It also became public knowledge that along with humble account customers, in its best times, the bank also had clients such as the sultan of Brunei, the Marcos family, Adnan Kashogi, Saddam Hussein, Alan Garcia, Daniel Ortega, Manuel Noriega, South American cocaine barons, the terrorist Abu Nidal, prominent leaders of the Islamic jihad movement, Libya, Syria, and the Mossad, as well as practically all the wealthy secret services. The IBCC apparently was essential in providing an outlet for heroin produced by Afghanistan and Pakistan. In fact, the bank's downfall began in 1989, when the activities of the Sakarchi Trading A.G., an investment fund based in Zurich, became known. It was accused of laundering some $10 billion in two years; the affair affected the Swiss Justice Minister, E. Kopp, and laid bare that one of the principal customers of the Sakarchi Trading A.G., along with Lebanese terrorist chieftains and other principals of unnamed businesses, was the CIA, with the objective of financing Afghan guerrillas, who were notorious opium producers.

The development of the IBCC in Spain, where it ended up having seventeen branches, indicates that its associates included a former Franco minister and the former ministers of economy and industry during the transition government. From 1981 to 1991, the Bank of Spain and the Fondo de Garantia lent it 21,400 million pesetas in loans, some of them without interest, and with exemption from the so-called asset coefficient, a dispensation that allowed it to increase its debt load and gave it freedom to invest at will. Naturally, those privileges did not prevent the bank from evaporating the deposits of some twenty thousand Spanish deposit customers.

We do not know what new international holding company now takes care of the interests formerly handled by Nugan Hand Inc. and the IBCC. But it must be an ever larger enterprise, which, like its predecessors operates under a cover of great respectability and solvency. To pretend that those finally in charge of operations are undocumented people like the Colombian P. Escobar, some Pakistani bandit, or a Burmese tribe is to confuse the smoke screen with what lies behind it.

According to 1992 estimates by the DEA, the yearly cash volume moved about by traffic of illicit drugs grew at the rate of $5 million per hour and involved the governments of almost forty countries (Afghanistan, Argentina, Australia, Bahamas, Brazil, Belize, Burma, Bolivia, Bulgaria, Chile, Colombia, Costa Rica, Cuba, the Dominican Republic, France, Guatemala, Haiti, Honduras, Hungary, Italy, Jamaica, Kenya, Laos, Libya, Mexico, Nicaragua, Pakistan, Panama, Paraguay, Peru, Poland, Syria, Taiwan, Thailand, and Turkey). Other nations simply laundered the profits

from a business shared by principal intelligence services, the ramifications of which had even reached the all-powerful American
National Security Council, going back to the time of "Irangate."
Since heroin, cocaine, and almost all designer drugs weigh less than
the paper money in which they are paid for, the postal services
transporting the money had to frenetically handle trunks loaded
with dollars, francs, and marks from airport to airport.

The Third World was already subject to tensions that operated
in the First World (police demoralization, dirty wars, immunity
of real dealers, etc.) that were aggravated by endemic poverty, and
had to fight against ancient traditions of moderate use and against
the only available means of making a living for many peasants.
The case of India is revealing, since it symbolizes a culture rich
in nonalcoholic means of inebriation from the very first Vedic
hymns. A fabulous opium production there during the nineteenth
century did not give rise to anything that could be called "abuse,"
and in 1981, not a single case of heroin addiction was reported
there. But in 1985, when the country accepted a harsh repressive
legislation to comply with international directives, the population began to substitute poppy juice for heroin, and in 1988, the
number of Indian heroin addicts, mostly young, was estimated to
be one million. Its neighbor Pakistan, with a much smaller population, had double that amount, according to the health minister
of the Benazir Bhutto government, whereas a decade earlier the
phenomenon had been largely unknown.

Legislative severity created paradoxical results in the Third
World as well. In Malaysia, for example, where the death penalty
was invariably applied to anyone possessing more than fifteen
grams of heroin, the government estimated in 1986 that there
were 110,000 heroin addicts—exceptional in a country with a
population of ten million. The same thing occurred in Thailand,
where the penalty was death or a life sentence but there were
about half a million junkies. The principal result of these
draconian laws was to create a monopoly of the traffic concentrated in a few hands, well infiltrated into institutions,
and excluding competition. Something similar was true in Latin

America, where—even though legislation drifted into harsh-ness—cocaine production in 1991 was a million kilos, something inconceivable twenty years before, and great land extensions were assigned to poppy cultivation.

In Europe, where illicit drug problems were largely unknown until the seventies, a persecution initially directed against psy-chedelics ended up being identified as a battle against the En-emy Within, American style, creating conditions favorable for organized bands around the hashish, heroin, and cocaine traffic. Starting at the end of the eighties, this traffic began to include MDMA and other design analogues. Criminality related to drugs had passed from being a negligible chapter to one encompassing three-fourths of all convictions, saturating prisons catastrophi-cally, multiplying by a factor of a thousand the involuntary deaths from fatal intoxication, and filling the streets with sellers and informants, paid with a percentage of what they turned in, whose intervention adulterated the product and at the same time assured its ubiquitous presence. News about substances that "disappeared" or "were reduced" after confiscation sug-gested that there was an informal tax, destined to support that dense layer of double agents, and that everything confiscated tended to end up, in whole or in part, in the black market. In Spain, for example, several high officials of the antidrug squads of the Guardia Civil were brought to trial accused precisely of that, and of having reintroduced some twenty kilos of cocaine confiscated through "informers."

The European black market was growing at a rapid rate, befitting a territory where the majority of illicit drugs carried no stigma for a considerable segment of the population, which included many young people, those marginalized by the system, and veterans from the sixties and seventies. Although the major-ity of governments generally lined up with the intransigent posi-tion favored by the United States, the example of liberal Holland was embarrassing because of the results it produced. The Dutch actually had the highest rates of illicit drug consumption but the lowest rates of fatal intoxication and related criminality, as well as the least correlation (6 percent) between the use of heroin and AIDS, when by comparison that correlation exceeded 60 percent in France and Spain. Dutch authorities explained their country's privileged position by the population's high awareness—instead of ignorance—of pharmacology, by the absence of counterproductive mythologies or alarmist reactions that distort the real effects of drugs, and by the availability of drugs through noncriminal routes. At the beginning of the nineties, several Swiss cantons adopted this position as well, even testing the free distribution of heroin to anyone who requested it, and making certain zones available for its consumption. The Catalonian authorities proposed to do the same in 1995, although the initiative seemed to have bogged down because of unforeseen obstacles.

The profound changes in this whole affair during the last few years reflected events taking place in the Vienna Convention of 1988, the aims of which were to stiffen penalties to the maximum and to confirm, on a global scale, several limitations to well-established civil rights, as well as to support other judicial irregularities: violation of privacy in domestic residences, mail, and telephones; obligatory analyses of urine and blood; longer times for proscribing penalties; automatic extradition; impunity for informants; exceptions to bank secrecy; prison and forced treatment for moderate users; approval of police purchase and distribution of drugs in order to discover dealer organizations; the right of police to resell for their own benefit a high proportion of assets seized from dealers; the right of police to provoke violations. Adapting international regulations to the American pattern, those implicated in illicit drugs were to receive the same treatment as terrorists, and police organizations had a free hand to do as they pleased.

The most controversial item in the 1988 convention was the "technique of watched transfer" (Art. 3), under which enforcement entities were allowed to promote the distribution of such products as long as they considered it necessary, in order to accumulate information about the black market. Some countries, such as France, passed legislation authorizing customs agents to "purchase, transport, and possess drugs during the legitimate exercise of their duties," which empowered them to "provide dealers with transportation, judicial means, warehousing, and communications." French legislation interpreted "judicial means" to signify the establishment of companies, the opening of bank accounts, and related activities. These regulations caused the release of six customs agents in Dijon and Lyon, convicted in 1991 for "purchasing, transporting, and giving away 535 kilos of hashish"—a conviction that assuredly provoked a nationwide strike by their labor union.

In other countries, such as Spain and Germany, the Vienna Convention proposals came up against hostile courts and judges, who considered them incompatible with basic principles of law, as well as a means to encourage and bless a galloping police corruption. Since 1990, the usual mechanisms of incrimination—by means of undercover police acting as gangsters or addicts who offer to buy or sell drugs—have come up against serious obstacles in Spain because of the doctrine of "provoked violation," where courts absolve the accused at the hearing phase when such methods are shown to have been applied. In 1995 a certain court not only absolved the accused but brought the police to trial, inaugurating a point of view frontally opposed to the directives suggested by the Vienna Convention. Several years ago, an organization called Judges for Democracy issued a proclamation against prohibition, outlining some concrete proposed legislative changes.

The reasons given by law, social science, medicine, and history against prohibition have not changed in the last thirty years, when Szasz, Becker, and Schnur, among others, diagnosed its probable route. Within strictly scientific circles, dissidence was—and continues to be—as unanimous as support for it appears to exist among political and religious leaders.

What has happened in the past decade, however, has given new life to the polemic, especially in the United States and Europe, to such an extreme that not only jurists, therapists, and professors openly declare themselves against the crusade but also police captains', mayors', judges' and district attorneys' associations, and high public officials including the prime ministers of some countries, such as Bolivia and Portugal. Even the Surgeon General of the Clinton Administration joined the opposition, although she was later sanctioned by the president, and the same thing occurred in the case of the drug czar in Spain, although Gonzalez, the prime minister, stated that that initiative was not part of his government's plan of action.

Unrest about the current situation has crystallized in several local and worldwide groups, which have the express aim of revoking prohibition. For the time being, the most active and well-known groups are the Drug Policy Foundation—led by the economist M. Friedman and the judge R. Sweet, as well as other notable Americans—and the International Anti-Prohibition League, based in Europe. Reversing the trend present in the past few years, surveys indicate that important percentages of the population favor legalization of the use and trade of all drugs, and in 1992, a referendum conducted in Italy obtained a favorable vote from 53 percent of the voters. Surveys are easily manipulated and for that reason not too trustworthy, but it would be reasonable to estimate that on the basis of those recently conducted, about 60 to 70 percent of adults—a higher percentage than that usually required to govern a country—already favor a new viewpoint on this whole subject. If public debate continues at a rate already evident in Switzerland, Italy, and Spain, for example, it would be possible for antiprohibitionist sentiment to reach and overcome the opposition, repositioning the matter before the mass public.

No one can foresee the reaction of such powerful forces as prohibitionist morals and the underground empire developed beneath it, tied one to the other inseparably, while diverging in ultimate aims. The future depends on their ability to face current unrest without modifying their basic premises.

We, who have in this book rapidly traversed millennia of universal history, consider the whole matter to have many hues. We know that the experiment has been to prohibit, and that no known culture, except for alliances exist between church and state, has ever granted governments a generic authority to rule over their "consciousness and states of mind," as expressed in the Agreement on Psychotropic Substances. When anyone alleges that any other route would generate an incalculable increase in drug consumption, let us contrast that conjecture with what we have learned in the past regarding penalizing them, legalizing them, or not making them fall under the rule of law. Now, as always, experiences count more than warnings.

Each one of us must decide whether the remedy is adequate for the ailment, worse than the ailment, or indeed the cause of the ailment. The Greek genius baptized drugs with a term *(phár-makon)* that simultaneously means remedy and poison, since one may become the other depending on circumstances, individuals, and knowledge. Whether drugs cure or do damage depends on human beings, not on drugs. Drugs have always existed everywhere, and judging by the present times, tomorrow there will be more drugs than exist today, so that the options are not a world with or without drugs. The alternatives are to teach people how to use them correctly, or to indiscriminately demonize them: to sow knowledge, or to sow ignorance.

Index

166 • *Index*